NO SMALL CHANGE

GLIMPSES OF GRACE IN THE ORDINARY

Charles E. Johns

CROSSLINK
PUBLISHING

No Small Change: Glimpses of Grace in the Ordinary

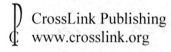 CrossLink Publishing
www.crosslink.org

ISBN 978-1-936746-21-7

FOR GAIL

"These last worked only one hour, but you have made them equal to us who have borne the burden of the day and the scorching heat."

–Matthew 20:12

"You'd be surprised the things I notice now."

–Tom Paxton, Folksinger

PREFACE

The beginning of *No Small Change* is time out of mind. The meal has been simmering in a slow-cooker with ingredients added all the while by family, friends, teachers, mentors, colleagues, encouragers, critics, clergy, laity, nature, art, cinema, poetry, music, scripture, tradition, reason and experience. They are the same ingredients we all use to name who we are, what we believe, and what is precious. As I begin to imagine thanking individuals it becomes clear that I am not prepared for a prime-time-high-wire-walk over the falls without a net. It is better to trust that the ones who nurtured me know who they are than to name some and forget others. In any case, naming would be far too long for this occasion.

To all my beloved friends who have added to this jambalaya, please believe that my gratitude is profound and, while your name is not written here, it is written in my grateful memory. I hope that I have already expressed my appreciation to you or, if not, I will be granted the time and opportunity to do it. There would be no meal to serve without you. We get by with the help of our friends.

I was nurtured into Christian maturity by the clergy and laity of the First United Methodist Church of Pittston. I had the privilege and joy of serving as pastor to the Throop United Methodist Church, the Moscow United Methodist Church and The Church of Christ Uniting (Kingston). These four Pennsylvania congregations have left their indelible faith imprint upon me and, consequently, upon *No Small Change.* I continue to drink from those wells.

Many of these reflections originally appeared as my monthly *Faith Matters* column published in *The Voice*, the newspaper of the United Methodist Wyoming Annual Conference between 1998 and 2006. After the print edition ended the column continued on the web edition of *The Voice* between 2006 and 2010. The Wyoming Annual Conference (Pennsylvania and New York) was divided along state lines and became part of the new Upper New York Annual Conference and the new Susquehanna (PA) Annual Conference in 2010.

All of the previously published pieces included here have been revisited, reconsidered and rewritten. Some that were previously published were beyond reclamation and transferred to an appropriate location. A number of new pieces were written for *No Small Change*.

For several decades I have been inspired by the writing of Frederick Buechner, Fred Craddock, Henri Nouwen and Kathleen Norris. My use of story, for which they are blameless, owes much to the way in which I experience their Gospel telling for our time. I have not had the honor to know any of them personally, but I am in their debt.

More recently, there has been a small but consistent band, the members unknown to each other, that has encouraged me to collect my writings and make them available to other readers. Initially I listened with one ear and, then, more recently with two. Their interest, encouragement and affirmation have been the tipping point to bring this collection together. I am grateful to John Bensinger, Sandy (McClure) Bensinger, Nancy Conklin, Gabriel Liew, Ann Mitchell, Donald Perry, and William Summerhill. Their confidence nurtured my persistence.

The Writer's Edge gave me the opportunity to set my work before those who might have an interest. It was a pleasure to be in their company for a while.

CrossLink Publishing took notice of *No Small Change* and has been an exemplary companion living up to their author-centric publishing ethic.

Last, but actually first, *No Small Change* is for my wife Gail, an extraordinary glimpse of grace in my life.

God's peace,

Chuck Johns

CONTENTS

INTRODUCTION

"Excuse me, Boss; I think you may have made a mistake. I just opened my pay envelope. The amount is right and that is fine. But you know that new guy who just started here late this afternoon. Well, I was near him when he opened his pay and he lets out this great whoop. I ask him what he is so happy about and he tells me. You know what? His pay was the same as mine. That is what I mean when I say there must be some mistake. You remember I came here first thing this morning and worked all day. I did not even take lunch or any coffee breaks. So how could the new guy get the same as me? He started work just before we quit. I know that you want to do what is right, so I just thought that I would bring this mistake to your attention. It is not fair and I know that you will want to ask him to return what he did not earn. Would you like me to send him in?"

We do not know much, but we know what is unfair. One of our most highly developed inherited traits, passed down from our Eden ancestors, is a particularly keen awareness of when we have been unfaired against. We respond pretty much the way the hearers must have responded as Matthew reports Jesus' parable.[1] The landowner's whimsy to pay all workers the same wage regardless of the number of hours worked strikes everyone as unjust. Jesus, master teacher, elicits from his hearers and from us the response he intends: "it's not fair."

It is an old conversation. It is a new conversation. It is an eternal conversation. I contend with God on a regular basis. Usually I plead my case when some injustice is perpetrated upon innocents by the authorities, by criminals, or by Mother Nature. I see unfair every day and I use the occasion to call to God's attention some abuse or other that I can't let pass without comment, question or recommendation. Most of my outrage comes when I see victims on the scaffold and corrupt power on the throne. I stand in a long queue before the Almighty to make my complaint. It is not fair that the innocents suffer what they do not deserve.

But then there are those occasions when I show my other face. I am not proud of my complaint, but I find myself standing in the other queue with my unfair list. But now, instead of a complaint about someone who has been abused, I am protesting someone who has been blessed. Using my own life as a measure, I can see unfair at every turn. It is not fair that there is blessing for those who have not earned it. I appear never to be satisfied with the way God runs things.

The depth and complexity of any parable defies a single interpretation. Here we can place ourselves within the story and stand with the landowner or the laborers. From where we stand, we respond accordingly. However, this is a parable for disciples, for only disciples can have any chance of entering upon the deeper meaning. One group receives their just wage and the other group receives an undeserved gift. We will visit this same point on another occasion when Jesus tells of a son who journeys to a far country to waste his inheritance.

This is not a prescription for labor relations. It is not an outline for a personnel manual. It is instruction for the faithful, for the church, and for the saints. It is a parable for all those of us who try to do our job well, tithe, make lime Jell-O for the funeral dinners, turn the other cheek, dutifully serve on boring committees, teach church school forever, let everyone else get in line before us, build houses for strangers, walk the extra mile, and rarely count the cost. The landowner asks the complainers "are you envious because I am generous?" Another way to ask it might be "do you think because I am generous to everyone it means that I value you any less?"

It is a reminder to those of us on the way that at the door of God's kingdom we enter with empty hands and empty pockets. The price of admission is nothing we bring, buy, earn, do, merit, accomplish, or achieve. The price of admission has already been paid and we stand at the door as the blessed. I have come to accept, understand and rejoice in that amazing grace. It is the bottom line of what I believe about God. At the end of the day it is where I lay me down.

However, here is the hard part. Here is why I understand that my conversion is incomplete. I still have my preferred distribution of God's grace. I am perfectly prepared to advise God on who deserves grace and who does not. There is a part of me that wants some reassurance from God that we all get what we deserve, what is fair. I would gladly advise God on how much each laborer should be paid based upon my judgment of their worth. I don't know much, but I know fair and unfair.

I can stand in both lines on the same day. Never satisfied, I protest innocent suffering in one breath and complain about unmerited grace in the next. I should hang a sign over my desk: weep with the wounded – rejoice with the blessed.

Some of us are slower learners than others. Because God loves everyone the same does not mean that God loves me any less. The grace of God is the gift of God's self. There is only one gift. God is the gift. Thank God, we do not get what we earn. Grace does not submit to the yardstick, scale or measuring cup. The primary truth that grace reveals about itself is not its weight, quantity, volume or price, but its presence. All the laborers get the same pay because God has no small change.

No Small Change sets out to expand an awareness of God's grace by pointing to the divine presence that we may not notice as we move through our days. I try to illustrate ways that readers might begin to acknowledge their own experience, reflect upon it and move beneath the surface to the source. To write about grace is to try to express the inexpressible. It is an expedition into that wonderland where we learn primarily by poetry and parable.

What follows are tales of people, places and things that can either pass unappreciated or can become elemental moments of definition. *No Small Change* is an invitation to pay attention to the grace that envelops and sustains us, that persistent Presence which longs to be embraced.

ADVENT AND CHRISTMAS

MALLED

It always seems much worse to me this time of year. Not that I ever covet mall shopping, but when the purchasing begins in earnest on Black Friday, malls are places that I religiously avoid so to speak. Always an introvert's *Purgatorio*, the mall now shifts into warp drive and issues a siren call to those on mission to make Christmas happen. I really don't want to be here but I am soon to learn that some epiphany has me on its radar screen.

Crossing the parking lot to the side entrance I notice that the gate to some fencing at a fast-food-drive-through is open enough for me to observe a man lifting the lid on a trash hamper. He seems to be looking for something. I try to imagine what that might be.

Mall faces are determined: lips tight and lines fixed. This is the land of hard surfaces. No one makes eye contact. Shoppers avoid one another. The popular songs of the season, sacred and secular, tumble haphazardly from the ceiling. I fall in line behind some seniors in running shoes who are tracking painted footprints on the tiles. I look long enough to wonder where the footprints will take me if I follow them. The moment passes quickly.

A grandmother, too tired to stand, sits red-kettle-side and rings her bell. She reminds those who have ears to hear that there is more to this festival than meets the eye. She keeps company with John the Baptist, a voice crying in the wilderness. She wishes me a "Merry Christmas" as I deposit my hope. The sound of her bell fades as I gain some distance from her proclamation. I begin to wonder if she is the reason I am here after all.

The price we pay for this season is high, sometimes too high for our own good. We spend so much time and money trying to perform Christmas that it slips away. What often remains after the Christmas high has waned is a question: "Is that all there is?" And even as the gift wrap is compacted into plastic garbage-sacks we wonder if we might have missed it again this year. Most of us know about Christmas disconnect.

Purchase made, I am leaving by a side entrance which I hope will have me in the same township as my car. I pause while a bailing-wire-duct-tape-bandaged beater in need of a new passenger side window struggles past. A gun rack in the rear window cradles a golf umbrella while a bumper sticker pleads: *God Bless America.* It reminds me, if I needed it, that this season also has an overlay of tears. There are empty chairs at Christmas dinner. The season of kettles and bells rings out for those who have nothing but their hope. It is the season of the longest night for all of us in this hemisphere, but it is much longer for some than others.

The church is no longer in sole possession of this season, if it ever was. Just now we are being urged to spend as much as we can to help rescue our economy. As usual, "more" is offered as anodyne. The season has its charms. For a few days we enjoy good will, good food and good music. But we have not learned how to outrun the longing that comes calling every Solstice. The longing speaks to us of our origins and our destiny. We are star stuff, light from light, bound to the creator for time and eternity.

John the Baptist, suffering in a cell, awaiting the judgment on his own future, sends two of his disciples to importune Jesus: "Are you the one who is to come, or are we to wait for another?"[1] John must answer his own question. We all must answer our own question. Jesus' response invites us to look at the evidence of our own eyes, listen to the evidence of our ears, and feel the evidence of our hearts. Tell John to look at the blind, the lame, the lepers, the deaf, the dead, and the poor for an answer.

That evidence is plain to the eyes of those who have recovered their sight. We are now the ones to live that evidence by touching, healing, reclaiming and reconciling. He invites us to use what we have been given. He promises us sight to see, ears to hear, and hearts to feel. It is hard work. It is holy work. In the pathways of the heart that story has become our story. We have been captured by its promise. And it has become our heart's desire to take no offense at Him.

As the mall recedes in my rear view mirror I am relieved to have it behind me. I am not fast enough, however, to escape being overtaken by the kettle grandmother's proclamation. I still hear her bell. I am not fast enough to escape her invitation to ring the bell that I find in my own hand. I take the long way home.

HOPES AND FEARS

I t is a tale of two cities. One is more a town, considerably smaller
than the other. Since time out of mind there have been ten
kilometers of separation between them. If it were not that they
frame the essential geography of our faith, they would be anonymous.
They are the cities of our purple seasons. We journey to Bethlehem in
Advent and to Jerusalem in Lent. They mark beginnings and endings,
birth and death, a room and a tomb, a choir of angels and an angel
solo, Christmas and Easter. They are two cities within an ancient
promised land that is home to us in ways we can hardly understand.

A few seasons ago, I made my first visit to Bethlehem to
experience that arcane mix of old and new, sacred and profane, in
which the Middle East specializes: soldiers at arms, Jews, Muslims,
Christians, peddlers with postcards, sidewalk shops with the bounty of
a fertile land, religious cliché for a price, religious truth and religious
fantasy and a mix of awe and aversion. The Church of the Nativity,
which dates to the fourth century, containing several sections claimed
by competing religious traditions, stands at the center. "Mine" and
"ours" mock the spirit of the Jesus they all claim to follow. The same
Lord grasped by competing factions, each convinced that they sit on
His right hand.

Tourists queue to descend to the lower level, the traditional site of
the cave where the Savior was born. There are smells of incense and
smells of people. There are sounds of Christmas carols sung in more
than one language, some I do not recognize. It was not what I
expected. It was not the Bethlehem of countless Christmas pageants.
Just another tourist, I should have known better. All of us waiting in
line are sisters and brothers in more ways than I can tell.

The liturgy of the day sounds from one or another of the chapels.
Pilgrims whisper as they drink in this place that lives in an imagination
painted by the pages of our King James Bible. Emotional, weeping,
trembling people patiently wait in line to get to their knees to kiss a
silver star, which tradition says marks the spot of the birth. It is a long
wait and it is a hard floor. How many kisses before these? And though

I do not kneel and kiss with them, I bend the knee of my heart. My silence is my offering. Silence is sometimes the best offering. If there were a little more silence perhaps we could understand something.

Bethlehem is not what I expected, but it is much more than I had imagined. Whether that one silver ornament embedded in the floor marks the precise birthplace or not, my heart sings the same song as theirs. Bethlehem stands for a timeless truth, a heart's desire, a light on all the dark streets east of Eden.

Philips Brooks, Rector of The Church of the Holy Trinity in Philadelphia, visited the little Arab village of Bethlehem in 1865 as our country began to recover from the Civil War and Lincoln's assassination. Three years later, back with his congregation in Philadelphia, he wrote the words of an exquisite carol which celebrates the timeless spirit of Bethlehem.

> *"O little town of Bethlehem, how still we see thee lie; above thy deep and dreamless sleep the silent stars go by. Yet in thy dark streets shineth the everlasting light; the hopes and fears of all the years are met in thee tonight."²*

We begin to imagine those hopes and fears. We could stand at the easel with newsprint and marker and fill a large sheet with our hopes and fears in parallel columns. We measure the distance between the place from which we have come and the place to which we are going. But then again the deepest of the hopes and fears are not accessible. We typically know them as the sighs beyond words, an unspeakable longing, and a restless desire to rest in God.

The hopes and fears of all the years is a song that plays within the deep center of all that we are, a tune we just can't get out of our heads or hearts. It is the national anthem of the peaceable kingdom. It is a profound desire for the healing of a broken humanity and the restoration of a disordered nature in the perfect order of God's reign. It is God's dream being dreamed within us. Hopes and fears are two sides of the same manger.

This purple season transports me once again. I am traveling to the Bethlehem of my hopes and fears. The little village is really a Shangri-

La of spirit, a hope-place where sighs, groans and longings are our prayers, where we kneel to kiss a silver star and arise to find ourselves on a street where the illumination is a little brighter.

By imagination I return to the cave with the silver star each year as the days grow shorter and the light fades. It is not the silver star that draws me back but the memory of hushed pilgrims on their knees shedding tears of memory and hope. The light from many candles unites the sound of carols and the fragrance of incense and humans in a tableau of hopes and fears. I bend my knee as fellow pilgrim, grateful for the grace that calls me here. I am at home in ways beyond knowing. There is still a light shining in the darkness and the darkness has not overcome it.

ANNUNCIATION

I set out to find one thing I think I need and end up being found by something else. The storage area under our inside stairs is an undiscovered country containing layers of geologic family time nesting in plastic, newsprint and bubble wrap. The lowest stratum harbors miscellaneous, unremembered shards, deposited time out of mind.

My goal was a compass that I wanted to use in conjunction with a topographical map. The compass had successfully hidden itself where dim light and even dimmer memory were no assets in recovery. As I excavated descending layers, I liberated a square package of some weight, wrapped in yellowing plastic, deposited at an earlier transition in my life. The parcel was a collection of a few dozen long-play vinyl records, musical fossils, hibernating quietly for many years.

I no longer have a turntable, my old-reliable long ago having refused any further efforts at rehabilitation. Many years ago I changed partners and began to dance with the compact disc. The records were voices from my past, vinyl preserving the soundtrack of my life. They would have their say. Music is a high wire act with no net, as risky as a high school yearbook.

A friend ("keep it as long as you want") entrusted me with a working turntable. I am self-taught in the process of transcribing vinyl to disc. Mysterious processes marry my records to turntable, amplifier and computer and, by some arcane magic, liberate voices muted by time and technology. Reluctant immigrant to this land of electronics, I learn the basic technique of media transcription. New occasions teach new duties. Sometimes new tools can teach old dogs new tricks.

The vinyl archaeology is time travel through successive layers of old passions: Welsh and Scottish folk music, the concert repertoire for solo flute, the humor of Tom Lehrer, the sound of exquisite music boxes, the Beatles *White Album*, folk singer Tom Paxton and Roger Williams' piano. The earliest layer, from my Bronze Age, was purchased more than one-half century ago. As I see the album jackets, I remember when, where and why I made the purchases. I remember

9

how much I paid. I listen to an LP and the vinyl unlocks memory's door. People and places are enlivened to cast their spell once again. I am reminded that whenever it wants the past can come and kick the door down.

What I assumed was forgotten is not lost, just standing quietly off stage, awaiting an opportunity to meddle. To listen is to hoist a sail with no clear destination. Music possesses the power to reveal secrets we keep even from ourselves.

Somewhere along about this time of the year, at the approach of the Solstice, I find myself in a new country without any awareness of crossing the border. Adam Smith's family has passed through customs before Halloween, juxtaposing pumpkins, skeletons and Christmas trees. But I know that I have entered into new territory because of the music I hear when the community gathers for worship. Plaintive plainsong gives voice to our longing for an advent promised by Jeremiah, Malachi, Zephaniah and Micah, fellow travelers in an ancient fellowship. The color goes purple as we set off across some of the same wilderness that we traveled in Lent. The music both evokes the longing and gives it voice.

Our advents parade in polite procession, linking us then and now to all humanity in our common need, regardless of our mother tongue. A song, too deep for words, refusing to be still, sings in our silence: O come, O come, Emmanuel. Something, someone, is trying to break into our lives once again. We think we know who and what it is, but we hesitate when asked if anyone in the lineup looks familiar. Poet Lawrence Ferlinghetti names this season for some of us when he writes:

> *Christ climbed down*
> *from His bare Tree*
> *this year*
> *and softly stole away into*
> *some anonymous Mary's womb again*
> *where in the darkest night*
> *of everybody's anonymous soul*
> *He awaits again*

an unimaginable
and impossibly
Immaculate Reconception
the very craziest
of Second Comings[3]

It is the season when the Angel of Annunciation comes to us in our fruitless expedition to find one thing or another we think we need, inviting us to sing the song that is within us.

Mother Mary stands in for us with the angel. She speaks our deepest need: an unimaginable and impossibly immaculate re-conception.

Let it be.

EPIPHANY

ASTROLOGERS

It is a mystery how the dust insinuates itself into closed drawers and locked cabinets. Microscopic fallout, talcum without fragrance, a gray glaze, comes to rest silently where it will. The airborne intrusion is a portion of the fee to be paid for the desired, happily imagined outcome. You do not serve a soufflé without breaking eggs. You do not amend the house without scattering some spackling dust. All of those seams, boundaries, and nail marks are made invisible and of one substance with the final wall. To attain that perfection, however, requires coveralls, eye protection, and a dust mask, not to mention a practiced hand. A Shop-Vac is not unwelcome.

Our happy dreams of grandchildren came true. When Alex and Owen visit they will need a place to sleep. A skilled carpenter translated our desire into footers, sills, studs, and rafters. It was a wonder and delight to watch nothing become something. It was the installation of the sheet-rock that posted the nuisance notice: ubiquitous dust. Comparable to the interstate detour, we took it as temporary inconvenience in favor of permanent improvement. It was the actual cost of travel to get to a desired destination. If we are not willing to accept the inconvenience of the journey, the destination will elude us.

We repack the Christmas decorations and transfer them to their resting place in the shed. We replace the Christmas music with the music of ordinary time. Shepherds and angels have returned to their own flocks. We open the door to the season announced by the astrologers. Alone among the Evangelists, Matthew tells of their mysterious travels.[1] He does not tell us how many there were. He does not tell us their names. He does not tell us their home town. He does not tell us their route. He tells us remarkably little. We are told of gifts offered to the Sovereign in a feeding trough and a furtive escape. A dream sends them home "by another way."

There was a wilderness to be crossed between the "East" and the place where the star rested. There is always a journey required to reach our destination. There is usually some Herod who wants to interrogate us. We return to a place that may well have changed since we left. As much as anything, the ancient, enigmatic star-seekers stand for the seeker within each of us. They leave the safety and comfort of their homes to travel to a foreign land, a deep desire their compass and a faint light their guide. It is little more than an itch and a promise: an invitation read by starlight.

Standing before the opening of one more year, we may hear some words of invitation: a journey, a fresh start, a new beginning, and an imagined future. This year we might finally be able to set some things down in favor of what we need to pick up. Some ancient urge lies dormant within us waiting to be awakened in this season of the longest night. It has all the earmarks of a journey to be sure, including its own inscrutable itinerary.

The mornings, remembered and forgotten, that I have set out in winter light to arrive at some self improvement, I have typically turned back before dark. In this game flesh holds a full house, spirit only two pair. The ante seems too high. Better to adjust to an address that is less than perfect than test our heart's true desire.

The deeper call, the one that moves us to follow an epiphany star, comes from a different location than New Year's resolutions. It is deeper than getting an application for a weight-loss program or enrolling in a course in time management. This is an invitation to a journey of growth in grace. With this reclamation, there is likely to be dust everywhere.

Like the anonymous astrologers, we sometimes respond to an invitation, a persistent inner claim upon us to live according to the reality to which we already belong. It is not in the stars this time but in the imagination of the heart. It is a quiet call to let become true what is true. It is a journey home, by another way.

RESOLUTIONS

I never tell anyone the resolutions I make for the New Year. When I invariably break them, generally before Epiphany, it is easier on me if I am the only one to know of my weakness. Failure at an interior level is enough to bear without adding family and friends. Actually, I rarely make any resolutions at the dawn of the year any longer. I might think about how good it would be if only I could take in more of one thing and less of another. I understand the impetus to look ahead to a new and better me as December becomes January. But resolutions, as far as I can tell, have never availed to make me a better person.

The problem I have found is that the kind of transformation I truly need and desire, inner change, is not amenable to resolutions, the obvious kind in any case. I say this from the experience of two-thirds of a century of trying to make it so. I resonate with St. Paul who laments that he can "will" what is right but that he cannot "do" it. The names of all those who nod in agreement with St. Paul are legion. If I cannot even balance my intake of protein, fat and carbohydrate, how can I ever imagine that I can make myself a "better" person, properly responding at the places where the road forks, discerning and doing truth in the moral ambiguity of the moment.

And yet, thank God, I am not the person I was. Looking back I can see that I have been changed over the years. I have a sense of going on, not necessarily to perfection, but to more compassionate responses to human need, greater patience with diversity, a clearer understanding of my own motives and desires, and a keener awareness of how I give myself permission to be selfish. Not any end point is in sight, but there is a desire to become a person of integrity, someone who wills one thing, one who's inner and outer selves are in harmony.

The changes have rarely been of my own making. I cannot say for sure how they have come, except to acknowledge that the Spirit has been about the silent work of reclamation. The people in the faith community that I trust, those I look to as models of Christian character, tell me something similar happens to them. We are being changed even though the specific awareness eludes us. Looking back I can see where I was, but I am not certain about how I got here.

But we are not only passive lumps of clay. We have played our role in the work as well. As far as I can tell, it has little to do with annual resolve or trying consciously to remodel our own interior landscape. I believe it has more to do with the focus of our attention, the use of our time and treasure, and responding to the call of our baptism.

We take our cue here once again from St. Paul who admonished the Philippians to think on things that are true, honorable, just, pure, pleasing, commendable, excellent, and worthy of praise.[2] We do have an active role to play in the shaping of our character. We become, it seems, like that on which we focus our heart and mind. We become, it seems, like the people in whose presence we delight. Like healthy plants we grow in the direction of the light shining upon us.

I have become more and more discerning and discriminating in what contemporary culture I allow into my life. A number of years ago I decided to stop watching television. I had become progressively disenchanted with its seductive appeal to all of the worst in us: greed, lust, violence, revenge, narcissism, and voyeurism. For good reason it has been compared to an addictive drug. Author Neal Postman writes of "amusing ourselves to death."[3] What I allow into my life shapes me.

But television is not alone. So much of what our society offers us by ear and eye and heart and mind does not build up but chips away at the moral sensitivity and values to which we aspire. The folks behind what we see and hear and read give us what we want. We are complicit with them. But it is my responsibility, not theirs, to decide what I allow into my dreams, my daydreams, my nightmares and my prayers. If I am not paying attention the culture will shape me its way. I begin to discover the power of renunciation.

Contemporary culture is not the enemy, just one tool of the enemy. The enemy is my own neglect of what is true, honorable, just, pure, pleasing, commendable, excellent and worthy of praise. These are moral categories more than aesthetic. "Think on these things," pleads Paul. He holds out for the Philippians and for us a means to an end. We are being urged to look through the window and consider before we open the door. Not all who wish to accompany us are worthy companions. Not all I see, hear, and read will take me in the direction I want to go.

Day by day I am becoming more and more like the people, places and things that I invite to share my journey. Although I rarely make any New Year's resolutions, there is a resolve within me, a restless yearning, a hunger for what is true, what is beautiful, and what is worthy of praise. I keep trying to make them my traveling companions.

TRUE COMPASS

As usual, I had convinced myself that what I wanted was also what I needed: a tool for a task and a solution to a problem. I searched the internet to evaluate a number of possible choices. I placed my selection on the family Christmas wish list, a worthwhile convention designed to reduce the number and variety of items destined for the church rummage sale. There are fewer surprises, but also fewer exchanges.

What I really and truly need is an auto compass. As I hesitate at two diverging roads it would be so useful to know the direction my choice will carry me. A compass would be a helpful Christmas gift, something that would get regular use and would get me to where I want to go. Typical of my gender, I prefer to arrive at my destination by obstinate determination rather than inquiry. Refusing to ask is another one of the signs of stubborn and prodigal independence.

Nesting inside the festive gift-wrap, the wish-list compass is packaged in silver, gray and black. It was manufactured in China. On the windshield, triune suction cups will anchor a handsome addition to my instrumentation, giving me the travel confidence I lack on unmarked roads. My first task, however, is to remove the instruction manual from the package and learn what I need to know about installation.

In many more languages than I ever hope to read, I am given far more information than I can ever hope to comprehend about where to snake various wires and sensors: altimeter, barometer, inside temperature, outside temperature, time, travel time, trip heading, photo sensitive backlight and, of course, a compass. I check to see if there is a transporter simply to beam me to my destination. I discover that I must calibrate the instrument by informing it of the latitude and longitude of my home base. I start to imagine adding a sexton to another wish list.

All I wanted was something to tell me if I was headed in the right direction: north, south, east or west. Will this particular blacktop take me where I need to go? The nuances of altitude, barometric pressure, temperatures, time and heading could be interesting information tidbits I suppose, but none of them will take away my ignorance at the crossroad. Multiple wires, sensors, buttons and an arcane multilingual manual of instructions bemuse me. I become frozen into immobility just pondering the installation. I got what I wanted but it was not what I needed. All I really needed was something to tell me which direction to go.

One of the things that Epiphany always suggests to me is direction. Ever since Matthew remembered that some unnamed astrologers from the East found their way to Bethlehem, it has been a question of direction. Not reluctant to ask for guidance, these seekers pursue a truth so profound that they must leave home to find it. At the end of the day they are lightened by the gifts they leave behind, they are wise enough to heed their dreams, and they choose an alternate route to their starting place. Starlight on their shoulders, they need to find another way home. I wonder if they found that home had changed since they left. When you find what you have been seeking, home may not be quite the same again.

Standing at the head of the New Year, a new decade, and a new journal page looking back at me, I glance both ways. In this season of the less-than-useful compass, still confusing what I need with what I want, I ponder the direction in which I have been traveling all this time. A star would help. On this road a simple compass would be a blessing.

The road always offers twists and turns, cul-de-sacs, and missing route signs. I still have the map in hand, although it is not without its ambiguities. I review my life-posts to see how far I have come from where I started. There has never been, and there never will be, any marvel of technology to release me from my choices.

What I do have are some fellow travelers who are headed in the same direction that I am. I have a few folks who help carry my backpack when it gets too heavy for me, some who tell me when it appears that I have taken a detour to the left or the right, and some who inspire me with their faith, hope and love. We worship, we pray and we work together along the way. I am grateful that I am not traveling alone. There is no way I could make this trip by myself. My traveling companions point me to the true compass. I give thanks for that wind rose for my life.

I carefully re-package the auto compass in its original silver, gray and black plastic shell. Gift in hand, I visit the giver and speak my thanks for his thoughtfulness and generosity. I apologize for the trouble to which I have put him. I ask if he would be so kind as to return it for me. I tell him that I really didn't know what I needed. He smiles a knowing smile. He has been here himself. We are both sure that we shall be having this conversation about what we want and what we need again before too many days.

FARM WORKERS AND STARGAZERS

Almost every church in Christendom has a few spare bathrobes so it is not so difficult, along with a few cardboard crowns, some wooden staffs and colorful scarves, to include all the visitors to the Holy Family in the annual Christmas pageant. We usually add a few sheep, some angels and perhaps a donkey as well. It is one of the best attended of all our advent rituals.

The first people on the scene were some farm workers who were taking care of sheep.[4] And talk about a special invitation. We are told that an angel was sent to tell them about the birth as well as telling them where to find the baby. And it wasn't just one angel. It was a Mormon Tabernacle Choir of angels singing God's praise.

Shepherds were the lowest of the low in that society. They were people from the project: no money, no education, and no prospects. They did the jobs that no one else would do. They were unclean. And for these 2,000 years the Christian Church has understood that God wanted them to get the first invitation. The angel choir ignores the rich and famous, the powerful, the priests and the Scribes and the Pharisees and goes directly to the farm workers, the people in subsidized housing who smelled like sheep. The good news of the birth of Jesus is first and foremost for the unwanted, the outcast, the marginalized, the used and the abused. Good news, the angel says, for you and for all people: a savior is born today. Get up and go and see what God has done for you. "For us? Wow!"

Sometime later, we don't know how much later, some wise men find the family and present their gifts. We don't know how many there were, we don't know where they came from, and we don't know where they went. [5]

The church has told their story for 2,000 years because it makes another very important point about the birth of Jesus. And the point is this: the Wise Men were not Jews, they were Gentiles. They were foreigners. They were from another country and another religion and another way of life. And that is the point: Jesus came not just for the Jews, although he did that of course. He also came for the gentiles, the foreigners, those outside the covenant. In other words Jesus belongs to the whole world.

So it is shepherds and wise men that get the first invitations. It is the nobodies on the one hand and the foreigners on the other who have the privilege of being first at the manger.

The shepherds and the wise men represent two different paths of the spiritual journey. The shepherds get the Mormon Tabernacle Choir and the wise men get a star. There are at least two different ways to God; two different ways to get home.

The shepherds are those blessed people who have had direct and personal religious experience. God meets them in some unmistakable way where they are convinced, convicted, once and done. They move through life with great spiritual certainly and with few doubts and seem to have answers to just about any faith question. They have been to the angel concert. God has spoken their name and issued them an invitation that they accepted. They smile a lot.

I know folks like this, and you probably do too. They have the spiritual life figured out and they radiate joy and peace. They have the bumper stickers that say, "I found it." God bless them. Some days I wish that it could be me. If I had a bumper sticker it would be more likely to read "Still Crazy After All These Years." Their patron saints would be the shepherds. They saw the angels face to face and they heard the sweet music of the night. And they are forever changed. If you are a shepherd, you have been greatly blessed.

But that is not everyone's story. That has not been my experience. I have had no private angel choir concert. I have not seen a burning bush. I have had no ecstatic visions. I have heard no voices. I have had dreams but they are always ambiguous and not enough to put my full weight down on. I have never spoken in tongues. I have never lost control of my feet during worship and danced up and down the center aisle. I have as many faith questions as I have answers.

Instead of that, I have been keeping company with the wise men. I have seen the star. I have been following that star for as long as I can remember. Sometimes the star is perfectly clear because there are no clouds and the moon is not full. But sometimes, like the wise men, I find myself crossing a desert. Sometimes along the way I have to ask people for direction. God has not sent me an angel choir but I swear I have met some angels. Often when I think I have lost my way someone comes along and gets me to look up again and see the star. And I believe that I am headed in the right direction even if I do not know a street address in Bethlehem.

I believe that there are at least two ways to get to Bethlehem. There are at least two ways home. There is the way of the shepherds and the way of the wise men. One is not better than the other. They are just different ways. God has a way for each of us.

And I imagine that there are others who might be on the stargazer road too. We meet shepherds and wise men and women along the way. And by God's grace we find each other and we tell our stories. We share our maps. We tell each other about the detours that we have taken. We mention the road blocks, the construction sites, the accidents, the toll booths and the scenic overlooks. We talk about the things that frighten us and the things that bring us joy. It is what fellow travelers say to each other.

Wise men and women may have bumper stickers too. They may not be quite as triumphant as some others. They say things like "Headed Home" or "Still Guided by the Star." But our assurance is real and our confidence is deep.

LENT

TOUR GUIDE

D esigned to capture the children's attention, the pastor's leading question was, "What do you think Jesus looked like?" The children, like chicks to mother hen, assembled in the chancel around her hips and ankles to see what she had up her sleeve that might surprise them on this Epiphany morning.

She produced a glossy-paged book that featured assorted artists' renditions of Jesus at familiar times in his ministry. In each case she asked the children's reaction to what they saw on the page. There was Jesus the good shepherd with a neck-scarf lamb, Jesus celebrating lilies-of-the-field in a verdant meadow, Jesus clasping a faithless Peter sinking like a rock beneath the Galilee, Jesus intense in one-on-one Gethsemane prayer and Jesus in the Jordan scanning the sky after the Baptist has fulfilled all righteousness.[1]

The responses were ones to be expected from children of the church. They had done this before. The young responses were all appropriate, predictable and orthodox. All save one that is. The young man on the pastor's right, chancel left, from all outward appearances disinterested in the proceedings so far, gave a nominal glance at a well-soaked Jesus at his baptism and pronounced, "He looks scared." A little child leads the way into deeper water.

Jesus looks scared. I'm not sure that possibility trespasses on my comfortable assumptions too often. I tend to read such confidence, control and focus into Jesus' mission and ministry that I rarely entertain fear as an option. In balancing the dynamic tension between the Jesus of history and the Christ of faith, I unconsciously have my thumb on the celestial side of the scale.

Out of the mouths of babes, a child invites us to entertain a more human Jesus, drenched with Jordan, God's pleasure assured, beloved status confirmed, and standing on tiptoe trying to imagine what this river water portends. Can he see the pale horse that will carry him to *ecce homo*? The dove has taken its leave. The wilderness beckons and his new companions become loneliness, hunger, thirst, temptations,

Old Scratch, fearsome beasts without and even more fearsome ones within. It is spiritual warfare behind enemy lines.

The prospect frightens me. I hope that it frightened Jesus as well. If it were no more than a walk in the park then it diminishes him as my chosen wilderness companion. I need someone whose fear is real because mine surely is. I need a decorated veteran, preferably one with a Purple Heart, to be my tour guide for the wilderness. Give me someone willing to lift a pant leg to reveal the scars; one marked with a red badge of courage.

A child senses the fear in this placid river scene. And when I look more deeply I sense it as well. The baptized beloved, affirmed by cosmic signs and wonders, knows that to be claimed by God is to set upon a mission that threatens the principalities and powers. It is to labor as an unwelcome, undocumented worker in a foreign land. St. Mark recalls that the Spirit "drove" Jesus into the wilderness.[2] It is a mission that must often be carried with little more than the memory of the water and the dove. We remind each other along the way that the seal upon us is indelible and eternal but we still anxiously glance about for some ministering angels.

Palm ashes on my forehead remind me that my ultimate destiny is in another's keeping. Lent is the community's offering of time to look full into the face of the dripping Jesus and, with him as tour guide, explore the fierce landscape of our soul. As one who has gone before, at the end of the day he stands among his friends and he says, "Don't be afraid."

Fear may well be one of the traveling companions of faith. We do not find our own way through the wilderness as much as we allow ourselves to be led.

PURPLE

I t is travel without first class accommodations. Transfiguration and resurrection mark the borders of this largely undiscovered country. We glance wistfully over our shoulder as the music of Mardi Gras fades to silence. It is a sparsely populated landscape. We respond to the seasons of the church year with degrees of notice, interest, and involvement. We have our preference and prejudice. The liturgical year resembles a travel catalog of spiritual destinations. We approach the ticket counter and book passage or we choose to wait for another tour.

Most of us eagerly await Advent and Christmas. It is a cultural carnival impossible to ignore. Various media introduce us to needs we never knew we had. The celebration is a welcome intruder around the solstice when darkness is about as deep as it is going to get. We sincerely hope for an everlasting light that "in thy dark streets shineth". It is a time for family, food, and festival. It is the season for which our bank will gladly open a "Christmas Club", financial preparation to balance the spiritual. Kris Kringle is Adam Smith with beard, pillow, and MasterCard. Christmas white covers Advent purple.

Just in time, the festival of Easter comes upon us when we have had about as much winter as we can bear. The fragrance of lilies and hyacinths, a lingering sun, and the consignment of woolens to mothballs invite us from hibernation, suggesting a rebirth of the earth and warmer joys. The commercial interests have not yet found a way to sell Easter, but not for want of trying: clothing, rabbits, flowers, and candy. The texts and hymns resonate deeply within and call us to hope in the face of contrary empirical evidence. We are refreshed, renewed, and returned to the front lines with the challenge of being Easter people. It is a season of "Yes."

The other purple season, however, comes knocking on our door like a homeless stranger seeking shelter. The Church has Lent to itself. There is scant commercial interest in celebrating a season of dust and ashes, fasting, scrutinizing the interior life, reassessing Gospel truth, and becoming a fellow traveler with Jesus as he decides for Jerusalem over Jericho. Still dripping with Jordan water, forty desert days and nights in hand-to-hand combat with the Father of Lies, the Beloved Son gets our reverent nod in prayers and hymns. However, we usually avoid eye contact, passing by on the other side, pulling up our collars, and hoping not to be recognized. Lent is generally that from which we pray deliverance. There is no need for extra chairs on Ash Wednesday.

The accumulation of years brings Lent into clearer focus for some of us. The festivals of Christmas and Easter, birth and rebirth, have been joys of bygone days. They will always be places we love to visit, rehearsing accumulated memories like prayer beads. We will warmly acknowledge them as beloved friends whose visit never fails to bring pleasure. Nevertheless, lately, as we approach the table spread for us, we notice that the Lenten cuisine claims a greater portion of our plate. Our tastes have changed. For those of us whose ship has not come in our hunger is not so easily satisfied. We entertain the possibility that less is more.

Raised in a community as one of a small Protestant minority, we staked our claim to truth by contrasting "our way" from "their way." The cross in our chancels was empty because we proclaimed a resurrected Christ, while our Catholic friends focused upon the crucifix, memorializing the suffering Christ. No ambiguity need apply here: simple truth for simple minds. Many Lents later, I begin to appreciate the symbolic and emotive power of Jesus hanging upon a chancel cross. To have my eyes opened even a little has revealed that the predominant state of humanity since our exile from the Garden is that of suffering. It is to that suffering humanity that the Lord of Life comes, "emptying himself, taking the form of a servant...obedient unto death, even death on a cross."[3]

Within the labyrinth of faith, death and resurrection are warp and weft, fibers woven into a single fabric, raiment for all the seasons of our life. Some of us are drawn to suffering as a way to seek the meaning of life. Some find the suffering Christ and the suffering of the children of earth a passage to enter into the heart of God. It is never a comfortable journey, but the itinerary holds the promise of hope's rebirth.

Purple does not flatter everyone. Purple is not always the color I choose. Lent is need more than want. Face set toward Jerusalem, Jesus continues to wait in the wilderness, inviting the willing to embrace his hunger and thirst for a suffering world.

MEDDLERS

Entering the side door of the Golden Arches, I did a rapid scan of the lunchtime crowd. There were four, roughly parallel lines of about equal length. I made a quick assessment of the one I believed would have me enjoying my salad and iced tea in the shortest amount of time. With no specialized training, I have mastered the dubious art of choosing the line that allows me to read one of the Pauline Epistles before my order is taken. I get more reading done in queues than I do at the library. This time I chose one of the inner lines, self-assured that most of my contemporaries would have deposited their trash before I finished my struggle with the packet of salad dressing. In the time-in-queue Olympics, I garner center platform and the national anthem more often than not.

With only one more customer preceding me in line, my attention was kidnapped by the conversation in the queue on my left. A customer had reached the cashier and asked to speak with the manager. The manager made his way to the counter and my curiosity became keenly focused upon what had called him forward. The customer proceeded to tell the manager that he and his wife were traveling through the area on their way to another town and they had not eaten since yesterday. They were hungry. The man wondered if the manager would be willing to give them something to eat. His wife was waiting outside.

The manager, no doubt, had been in this situation before, perhaps many times. As a matter of self-defense, I imagine he had practiced a response to any and all such requests. The manager was not unkind but he was firm as he told the man that he could not help him. He was not allowed to give food away. The man asked again saying that he would be happy with anything the manager was willing to give. It did not need to be anything fancy. The manager again said that he was "sorry" but remained resolute. He appeared to be embarrassed by the situation, but apparently powerless to change it.

Something about this drama overwhelmed me. Conscience stricken, I was unwilling to allow the man's request for food to be denied. Without any conscious decision to do so, I stepped out of line and moved to the counter where the manager and man were speaking. The words that came from me were, "please give him whatever he wants and I will pay you for it." I spoke quietly because I did not intend to call any further attention to the interchange than had already been called. The manager was nonplused but he told the casher to take the man's order. After receiving my own lunch, I waited at the end of the counter for the manager to tell me what I owed for the strangers. The man received his food, nodded in my direction, and made his way outside to join his wife. When the manager approached, I asked what I owed for the food. He said that I owed nothing. He had taken care of it himself. I thanked him. The strangers were nowhere to be seen.

My part was no great thing to be sure. It cost me nothing as it turned out. It cost me only my willingness to address an unacceptable situation that was in my power to change. I did not engage myself in a debate about whether this was the "right" thing to do, or whether the man and his wife were just trying to get a free lunch, or whether the manager was a good person or not. There was no need: someone was hungry and I could do something about it. It took no brain and just a little heart.

The lunch incident invited itself into my awareness and then stayed on for days after that meal. It had the effect of calling to my mind, not other situations when I had acted in a similar way, but rather the opposite. I began to remember other times and places when I was faced with an unacceptable situation that was in my power to address and, for whatever reason, I did not. These inner journeys can be as painful as they are instructive. Unintended excursions into memory frequently open doors we have locked and turn on lights that cast shadows in dark places. We can be equally taught by what we have done and by what we have failed to do.

By our baptism we Christians are initiated into a family of meddlers, some might even say troublemakers. As part of the process of growing into our baptism, we develop sharper eyes, keener ears, clearer voices, bigger hearts, open minds, open arms, and empty hands. Some of the most transparent teaching we have from Jesus regards the neighbor. Minding our own business is never a settled option in this family. To love mercy is a gift, not an achievement, and no reason for pride. God knows, even with the purest of intentions we frequently get it wrong. For our part, we are urged to act upon what we believe to be mercy, receiving mercy in return. It is often simple, rarely easy.

Mid-season-lent, the equinox comes into view, the passion is still clothed in purple, and we are reminded of the consequences of God's incarnation in human history. We ponder God's incomparable, merciful meddling that will have its way with us. Overcome by that mercy, we receive our vocation. We stand in line to place an order for one kind of meal and end up being served something else.

HOSANNA

The hill is always steeper than I remember. I brace myself to keep control of my descent. My gaze is transfixed by what is on the other side of the valley. There, in magnificent and terrible splendor, lies the Holy City, Jerusalem, a stone's cry from the Mount of Olives. There is no other city on earth that claims me so. By invitation from the Psalmist, the Israeli army checkpoints in view, I add my aching, timeless prayers for its peace. How long, O Lord?

I try to imagine the palm-waving crowd. Hosanna! It is a proclamation and a plea: "save us."[4] Of course, he knew what was going on. To wave a palm branch was the equivalent of waving a flag. It was a political statement, a suppressed people crying for release. "Hosanna" means good riddance Rome. The wavers, who could blame them, were hoping that this was David's promised child, liberator at last. The stories had arrived in advance of the rabbi on the donkey. Others had failed, perhaps he would succeed. It was worth a shot in any case –any port in a storm.

The steepness of the hill has my legs protesting. At its foot I reach my destination. Once a garden where oil was pressed from fruit, it is tonight a desert where blood, sweat, and tears are pressed from human flesh. He has shed more tears over that city than he cares to remember. He is well to wonder if anyone within its walls will return him the favor at week's end.

Hard as it is to descend that hill, it is far more difficult to summit. We claim the week "holy" with such mixed emotions. We begin the week in the triumphant, ironic truth acclaimed by the crowd: "Blessed is the one who comes in the name of the Lord." They did not know what they were saying. We end the week in bitter disappointment. He does come in the name of the Lord, but his coronation is his crucifixion, his throne a cross, and his devoted subjects are a few women and two criminals. He is less than we project, but more than we can imagine. But if not the crowd then the stones would shout the truth. Sometimes the stones are wiser than the people.

I endure the gauntlet of peddlers, postcards, beads, and olive wood crucifixes impeding my pilgrimage. I resent their interference here. But it was little different then. It is less a question of what is being sold here and more a question of what we are buying. As always, he comes to us in the midst of life. The peddlers have their role to play in this drama now as then.

Some say that the very trees behind the iron fence were there when he prayed that the cup would be withdrawn. Rocks and trees bear silent witness to that Thursday night. Disciples are often sleeping at critical times. I glance back up the hill and remember that this was a one-way trip. Behind the walls of the City of Peace there is an appointment with destiny.

Three times he allows God the opportunity to find another way. Three times he prays. Three times they sleep. Three times one of them denies that he even knows the hosanna man. Sweat and blood, blood and sweat, who can tell the difference? Next to the garden there is now a house of worship. The Basilica of the Agony is well named.

But now it is settled. "Let us be going". There is a time to pray and a time to act. There is a time to shout "hosanna" and a time to shout, "Crucify." There is a time for acclamation and a time for desertion. There is a time for promises and a time for lies–a time to live and a time to die. A faithless kiss, the kiss of death, becomes the hope of new life. His asks his disciple to put aside his sword.

One washbasin away from a cross, judged by those who do not understand, *ecce homo* remains silent. Around high noon on one very Good Friday, in a terrible beauty, the hosanna prayer is answered.

CONFESSION

Even as she walked down the front stairs of the church with her back to me, it was clear that I had failed to change her mind. While shaking my hand and her head, the woman told me that she was uncomfortable in our worship services. She was not critical of the length of service, music, preaching, announcements, babies crying, clapping, talking during the prelude, or lapses of the public address system. Rather it was because we used corporate prayers of confession. She said that they were too "negative" for her. Confession was a turn-off. She cited a well-known television preacher to bolster her argument. She came to worship for a positive, uplifting experience and our prayers of confession took away some of her joy. She intimated strongly that, unless we abandoned our practice, she would need to worship elsewhere.

In the few seconds allotted for such seminars, as others impatiently queued behind her, I gave an abbreviated theology for our use of prayers of confession. It was clear that she was unmoved by my eloquence. I invited her to sit and talk with me so we could have the luxury of time to learn from each other. It was an offer she was able to refuse. If we were to poll the average congregation I strongly suspect that she would find not a few fellow travelers. They would likely stand in company with those who do not warmly embrace the doctrine of original sin.

One of my longtime ecclesiastical maxims is that people need to worship and serve where they are spiritually nurtured. And while we would like to believe that we can satisfy all hungers in our congregation, we know that only God can do that. It is painful for pastor and congregation when a worshipper finds the service wanting. It is a humbling experience to be found inadequate in this way. It is painful when the person departs to find another congregation where they can be fed. But faith communities discern differently and they cannot satisfy everyone at all times. Patience quickly fades in a culture where we can sample another offering with a mere click of the remote.

That front-door epiphany has lingered for many years. Not only was I taught a lesson about liturgical preference, but it also strengthened my conviction that corporate confession is an integral part of worship. Confession opens our past to the light, recalling the deeper truth about ourselves in order to expose our souls to healing grace.

Now I know that much of what passes for confession in our orders of worship is perfunctory. The written prayers often ask us to identify with the most pernicious sins in the most general way, and that within about fifteen seconds. The time for silent confession, like other times of silence in worship, remains only until the first person begin to cough. And yet spoken and silent confession is a critical signpost on the way, pointing the direction to God's presence. The Sunday confession plants the seed for a deeper exploration when the Spirit leads us to it. It reminds us that "in the name of Jesus Christ we are forgiven." It is the promise of a lifeline to which we may cling whenever our past comes calling.

To remember is to give thanks for what is good. To name that grace bonds us to the God who is its source. That grace makes us smile, but it also makes us weep. The grace is by definition undeserved and unmerited. To remember grace is also to face how we have failed to live in that bounty and, if necessary, ask forgiveness for ourselves, our community of faith, our nation and our human family.

In my own journey I have learned that when I neglect the remembrance of my failure, when I avoid facing the plain truth about what I have done and what I have failed to do, I leave a barrier between myself and God, myself and others. When I am content to drink from a tainted cistern my thirst is not quenched. When I refuse to deny the past I can interrupt its power to sabotage my future. The deadliest sins of all are the ones not confessed. Their power over us is broken when they are named and owned. Far from being "negative", it turns out to be liberating, joyful and live-giving. The invitation by God to confess is an invitation into grace, peace, and hope.

Lent, our other purple season, brings all of this to mind in a more focused way than usual. Invited to remember and surrender our past to God, we are being prepared to accompany Jesus on his way. He is still damp with Jordan and we have a smudge of ashes upon our foreheads, fellow travelers through the wilderness, and companions on the way to embrace God's future.

WRONG NUMBER

She believed she was speaking to an answering machine at the fuel-oil company. Her accented, anonymous voice sounded young and desperate. She reminded my voice mail that we had delivered oil to her last week but today the furnace was not working. They had no heat in the house. She recorded her telephone number and asked that someone call her as soon as possible. "It's freezing," she pleaded.

My outside thermometer registered a bitter single digit with a wind chill south of that. I shivered as I thought about her. I pictured rural mobile homes huddled together on exposed acres trying to warm themselves like cattle in a storm.

I began to wonder if there were children or elderly with her. It was not difficult to imagine myself in her place and to consider the damage that a single digit could do to water pipes, not to mention the health of a family. I called the telephone number that she had left on my machine. At least I could tell her that she had reached a wrong number. I could let her know that she would need to make another call if she wanted her furnace repaired.

After a few rings an electronic voice informed me that the number I had reached had no human to answer. I listened to my voice mail once again thinking that I might have heard her number incorrectly. Sadly, the number she spoke was the number I called. I tried once more only to be greeted by the same indifferent voice with flat affect: "no longer in service". It seemed she had neither telephone nor furnace. How had she called me in the first place? How did she get my number?

My imagination failed to reveal any additional way for me to intervene on her behalf. I wanted to help change this situation but I could not see how. I could not fix her furnace but perhaps I could help her reach someone who could. If I could just talk to her there may be some way I could make a difference.

I received no absolution just because it was a wrong number. I hoped that she would try again and this time she would get the right

42

number. I thought of others who were shivering that morning. I reflected upon how a wrong number had troubled my comfort.

The anxious, accented voice spoke for countless others in my experience who shiver in their need. It is often the solo voices that take up residence within us. Voices with a face, voices with a story, and voices without other places to turn for relief or rescue make stronger claims upon us.

In these days anonymous multitudes in faraway places with strange names suffer from one kind of terror or another. Bullets call and bombs answer. Bombs call and bullets answer. There are countless answers without questions. There are wrong numbers all around. In addition to human on human violence there are always earthquakes, hurricanes and tornadoes that level cities without regard for the moral worth of the residents.

Unable to change human nature or nature's nature, a feeling of powerlessness mitigates our response. We desire to return the call, to intervene, but often learn that no one is answering. A citizen plea for justice or a charity check for relief often seems to be blowing against the wind. But blow we must and blow we do. One hand lights one candle and one heart sighs a prayer too deep for words. We hold prayer book in one hand and check book in the other.

The far away voices, victims of human or natural mayhem, are easier to bear than one anxious voice on our answering machine. We make our easy peace with conscience the greater the disaster, the greater the distance. One voice, one face, one story grasps our lapels with firmer grip and will not let us off so easily. We find ourselves returning the call.

Luke, alone among the Evangelists, remembers Jesus weeping over Jerusalem, anticipating his destiny within its walls. "If you, even you," he cries, "had only recognized on this day the things that make for peace! But now they are hidden from your eyes."[5] His are the tears of helplessness. He knows that he will be unable to make Jerusalem live up to its name as The City of Peace. He sees for the city what it cannot see for itself. The truth conveniently disguises itself or is so painfully transparent that it must be denied or discounted. He calls but no one is answering.

At the last he does what he can, indeed, what he must. He boosts himself upon the colt and turns his face into the wind on a one-way road. He is brother to us in our helplessness. He is brother to us in our hopefulness. He is brother to us in our doing.

Truth to be told, when wrong numbers connect us with need, sometimes they become the right numbers. We turn our face into that wind and may well discover that we are God's answer to somebody's prayer.

TIME TRAVEL

Making the right turn after the stop sign, even without seeing, I knew something was wrong. The house was gone. It had been home for me about as far as memory reaches. We never owned the house. It went with the job. The people who came after us loved the house far less than my parents did. A pile of rubble now marked the place, no challenge for the bulldozer to collapse the tired old wood. The broken bits and pieces were unceremoniously loaded to dump trucks for their final journey to the landfill.

A few lengths of pipe stuck out of the cellar like compound fractures through a broken leg. There was the stump of the large pine that had shaded the porch for close on to a century. What was once forty feet of stately green and endless cones was now an eighteen inch dwarf. Walking the ruins, remembering the floor plan, I felt a refugee, homeless, even though I had been absent for years.

I cast about to find something familiar amid the ruins. My eye fell upon a shard of green asbestos siding. It had been a major event in my young life when that siding was installed in the early 50's. I rescued the scrap of brittle board, brushed it off, and secured it in my jacket pocket. I keep it in the desk drawer in my study. I open the drawer to retrieve the stapler and it sits there and speaks to me. In eloquent silence, it recounts nearly a half-century of family life.

It is just a piece of old siding, but it possesses evocative power. To hold it is to be a child again in that house. To touch it is to embrace parts of my story that seem otherwise to be forgotten. It is not a magic charm. I do not believe in magic. It is concentrated memory, distilled time. As an icon, it has the power of the tangible to release the intangible, making the present transparent to the past. For a few minutes I am visited by a sacred spirit of place.

We are our memories. Sometimes memories can be unreliable vagrants. Often the simple and the serendipitous can animate them. A few bars of music, the words of a song, the smell of cooking, a whiff of perfume, the taste of a Christmas cookie, the touch of asbestos siding can transport us immediately and powerfully to forgotten people and places. Time travel is a reality. We laugh or we cry as if we are there. By memory we are.

The Christian faith is a life of remembrance. It is a life of recall. We gather as the community to hear the story repeated. The story tells us who we are. We become part of that story. In remembering the story, we come to faith once again in the present.

St. Paul writes to the church at Corinth and tells them what he remembers about the Holy Meal, what was remembered by those before him and passed down to him.[6] He rehearses the word from Jesus that invites his disciples to "do this in remembrance of me". Remembering is so critical to the disciples of Jesus that it is no less than the Holy Spirit who is entrusted with the work of making it so. When we forget we are cut off. When we forget we are lost. Someone with amnesia has no past and therefore no present.

For two thousand years, our extended family has preserved and retold the story of that Holy Meal. It is the story that the Church tells to help us remember and understand what God has done for us. Through the eyes of love, we are empowered to participate as a community in the first meal long ago, participants in the whole wondrous story of salvation. It is much easier to forget when you are alone. The community cannot let us forget.

We hold that bit of bread in our hands, we look closely, and it takes us in. The sip from the cup touches our lips and we know that the vintage is timeless, the sweetness of an unspeakable joy without end. By the Spirit's power of remembrance, it is not just First Church Sunday morning any more than a broken piece of siding is just what remains of a beloved old house.

By remembrance, in the power of the Spirit, the bread and the wine transport us to that table where the host once again re-presents himself, offering the signs of life and life eternal, anticipating the meal without end, the supper of the heart.

GARDENS

There are stories that frame and interpret our lives. There are sacred and secular texts that write and re-write us. They are the stories of our time and place, where we exist and where the most precious things are kept. They are stories about emotion and conscience, memory and intellect, sensation and intention. They are our stories. We are the performers and we are the audience. The stories are frighteningly public. They are mercifully private.

Lent is an invitation to remember some of our stories. The days are getting longer, the winter solstice is past, the vernal equinox is soon to make her entrance upon stage, the seed catalogues are in the mailbox and the over-wintered bulbs nudge through frost and snow at the sun's urging. The strains of Mardi Gras fade to silence as the band packs up their instruments for the ride home. The promise of rebirth is just over the horizon even if not yet in sight.

Inside the sanctuary the lights are low; the organ is subdued. We sit and wait while Hosanna ashes are mixed, bread is broken and wine is poured. We have been here before. The colors change from green to purple. The pulpit voice is in earnest. The Psalmist calls to the Almighty on our behalf to "blot out my transgressions, wash me thoroughly from iniquity and cleanse me from my sin."[7] Lent begins as we are admonished to sit up straight, wipe the smiles from our faces and pay attention. We are dust and ashes true enough. We live on borrowed time. But we are also those who partake of the divine mystery by what is broken and poured. Once again here tonight we are reminded that old futures are gone. We drink to that promise

We are invited to hear the Word of God from Genesis. We are reminded that in the beginning there was mystery, void, and silence. We are told how that changed when God speaks: nothing becomes something, something good. The right word changes everything. And there was a garden. And there was a choice. The words garden and choice are enough for those of us who have visited Eden before. Two words stand in for many. We remember well both the delights and dangers of that lovely place: a whimper, a separation and an eviction.

47

Eden can prove an undoing. The first gardeners discover their nakedness and become strangers in a strange land.

I accept an invitation to remain in this garden for while. I spend a few moments with the first Adam in Paradise. Standing before the one and only tree with consequences, he ponders whose way rules him. He chooses his own way and in his free choice he is turned out. He weighs one promise against another and rolls the dice. Like our first father and mother in the alpha garden, the apple does not fall far from the tree. We have no way to free ourselves from the bondage to our own will. My will be done. My address is east of Eden. It is why we need a savior. The first garden and the first parents are written upon my forehead in a black smudge. This is my story too.

But the liturgy of the day is not through with us. Ashes are replaced upon the table, fingers are wiped clean and other things are taken to hand. As soon as I see the bread and wine I can taste them. It is a foretaste. Wonder Bread and grape juice have a garden story to tell and they will have their way with me. They are the other side of ashes. I accept the invitation to visit that other garden too.

The second Adam spends his last night alone in the place of the oil press and ponders the same choice as the first. Sweating blood, he prays for some other way: too young to die. Like other men he might well have dreamed of a wife and children. He could have imagined opening a carpenter shop with the tools his father left him. Peter could teach him how to catch fish. Would it be such a terrible thing to change his mind? People do it all the time.

But, instead of holding out for better terms, he opens his hand and the fruit falls harmlessly to the ground. The serpent slithers away. He lifts the cup to his lips and drinks. History is undone. Inevitability is cancelled. The gates of the garden are unlocked and thrown open.

There is a tree in both of those gardens. One tree grows in paradise. The other stands outside the city on a garbage dump. One tree promises knowledge, the other life. Paradise or garbage dump, apples or grapes, seem of lesser consequence than the choices that are made in the shadow of those trees.

We are adjourned from the Wednesday of ashes to the awareness of night air, unfinished business, and miles to go. The ride home is interrupted at the first stop light by a question opening the door and getting into the passenger seat: how will I choose between the trees that grow in my garden? It is so hard to tell those trees apart. One choice leads to what appears to be life and turns out to be death. Another appears to lead to death but really turns out to be life.

We have been to Eden and we have been to Gethsemane. They are the same garden. It just depends upon how we choose. I become aware of the smudge on my forehead. I become aware of the taste on my lips.

HOLY FIRE

"Where are you, good Jesus, why were you not here to heal my wounds?" A despondent cry echoes from the sixteenth century. It is the cry of the abandoned in every age. In this case it is the inscription that accompanies a painting of St. Anthony being tormented by monsters and demons in one of the panels of Matthias Grunewald's Isenheim Altarpiece.

Killer plagues terrorized Europe regularly in the middle ages. St. Anthony's fire, a disease now known as ergotism, was caused by the poison of a fungus and spread by tainted rye flour. The terrible scourge was sometimes known as "Holy Fire." Without knowing its source and without any cure the serial killer had nothing to impede its mayhem. Descriptions from the time speak of the boils on arms and legs that rapidly developed into abscesses along with nervous spasms and convulsions. Painful skin eruptions blackened and usually turned gangrenous, often requiring amputations. It was a devouring monster, rivaling an extraterrestrial alien nightmare, which literally consumed the body in excruciating pain. This monster, however, was mercilessly real.

The monasteries of the time provided about the only anodyne available. In their "infirmaries" they offered prayer and plants as they had to ease suffering. They offered the sacraments of the church and human compassion in the face of Holy Fire. Dauntless monks faced down the killer in hand-to-hand combat in the dark. It is courage and mercy that still inspires us. It is a fight to the death with no holds barred, no quarter given and against all odds. The Order of St. Anthony kept a hospital in Isenheim primarily for those who contracted the Holy Fire. They took their name from St. Anthony, venerated as both a sufferer and a healer; a pioneer in monasticism.

Matthias Grunewald, a well known artist and engineer, was asked to take an existing altarpiece of wood carvings and to paint an extended altarpiece for the chapel in the Monastery of St. Anthony in Isenheim. He completed the work between 1512 and 1516. Many art historians believe the altarpiece to be an artistic creation which rivals the *Mona Lisa* and the ceiling of the Sistine Chapel. The altarpiece is now in a museum in Colmar, France.

The center panel of the altarpiece, the artist's view of Golgotha, is considered among the greatest ever painted, a masterpiece of northern Renaissance art. You realize you have never ever seen a rendering of the crucifixion of Jesus like this before. It is a horrific nightmare of Calvary. A beaten and bloody Jesus on the cross is horribly twisted and contorted in pain. We might imagine how a victim of torture might appear. He is pulled down by an invisible weight. His open palms, nailed to the cross bar, reach toward heaven in supplication, as if he bears the sin and suffering of the whole creation. If you stay with the painting a little longer you will see what is weighing him down. Jesus' body is covered with the ulcerated, gangrenous sores of St. Anthony's fire. Jesus is a victim of the Holy Fire.

Grunewald shows Jesus entering into the suffering of those desperate, suffering victims. The artist asks, "Where are you, good Jesus?" and then answers his own question. The artist takes his stand with Isaiah: "Surely he has borne our infirmities and carried our diseases."[8] The creed affirms, "He descended into Hell." The artist invites us to share his conviction that there is no length to which the love of God will not go to save us. The central panel was positioned in such a way that it could be seen by the suffering, dying patients in the monastery infirmary.

Before we get to the Easter lilies there is another station where this train must first stop. On the last night of his life Jesus shares a meal with his friends and asks them to remember him in his body broken and blood shed. We remember him in his vulnerability, his self-offering, and his descent into hell. We remember that for our sakes he was willing to be as far away from Abba as the beloved child could be from the parent.

In the ulcerated sores of St. Anthony's Fire on Jesus' body Grunewald reminds those with eyes to see that the Christ is found wherever the fires of hell are burning. No suffering is exempt from God's presence. It is a parallel journey that the family of Jesus takes whenever they choose to stand with the victims of whatever Holy Fire happens to be calling itself these days.

IN THE DARK

The lights went out. It is not an uncommon occurrence where I live. Country living makes some accommodation to urban certainties. Experience has taught us to have auxiliary lighting at the ready. The last time the power failed compliments of snow, ice and wind, the unexpected darkness was an opportunity to remember another time when the lights failed for millions of us.

When I remind you of the evening of November 9, 1965, if you were of a certain age, you will likely recall it. That was the night of the "biggest blackout in history." The entire northeastern part of the United States was plunged into darkness for several hours. Some 30 million people played out their respective roles in an extemporary drama written by a power failure. That evening's events, good and bad, bookmarked the people and places around those of us who were there. If you were there, you will probably recall what you were doing when the power failed that night.

The night of that blackout I was part of the congregation at an installation service for the new Rector at an Episcopal Church in upstate New York. The Collect for Purity of Heart was still on our lips when the light flickered once and then disappeared entirely. The blackout, while not unnoticed, was of little consequence for us. The organist moved to the piano while we lighted the many candles already in place. It was quite luxurious to be baptized in that soft, flickering light.

Friends and strangers moved closer together to share the light and warmth and to make our several promises before God and each other. We sang and prayed God's blessing upon our brother who was being commissioned to shine in the darkness. You could do a lot worse than to find yourself in a sanctuary during a blackout. Churches are typically better prepared to continue in the dark than many other venues. We recall those unfortunates who spent the evening passing the peace in elevators and subways.

Some time ago I read that Vladimir Horowitz, one of the greatest pianists of our age, was playing a rehearsal for some guests in advance of a concert that night in Carnegie Hall. He had just begun to perform the Chopin *Polonaise-Fantasy* when the hall went black. He continued playing without missing a single note. After a short time he stopped to discover from a stagehand that the power was out all over the city. He said that he did not mind playing in the dark if the audience didn't mind listening in the dark. The stagehand brought out a candelabra and the concert was played to completion.[9] Horowitz could play incomparable music in the dark because he had practiced his music in the light. He and his music were of such a unity that light and dark were the same to him.

St. Luke tells us about that day the lights went out in Jerusalem.[10] It was some time after high noon one black Friday at the place locally known as "the skull", a first century killing field. Three condemned criminals were being made public exemplars of Roman justice: capital punishment as political education. Luke remembers a three-hour blackout. The sun's light failed or was eclipsed. The dirty business of death by suffocation is made all the dirtier by darkness. Luke took it as celestial comment upon the proceedings. It seemed almost as if it were too painful for the Almighty to look upon in full light. God turns aside, as it were. A descent into hell, affirms the creed.

Luke further testifies that he heard the criminal in the center, the teacher, offering his spirit into God's hands at the last. Jesus entrusts his spirit, his life, his work, his ministry, his death, and his all-in-all to God in the dark when the lights were out. He could hand himself over in the darkness because he had already presented himself in the light.

He had practiced that submission day by day ever since he walked into the wilderness wet with Jordan. The Gethsemane submission last evening made this day both possible and inevitable. He and Abba were of such a unity that light and dark were the same to him. "For darkness is as light to you," is the Psalmist's timeless illumination.[11]

We could commission a pastor in a little church in upstate New York in 1965 when the power failed because we had all the light we needed in our shared candles and all the warmth we needed in our huddled bodies.

Horowitz and Chopin were on such intimate terms that even in total darkness the pianist could see the keys and hear the music.

Composer and performer were of one mind. The lifetime they had spent together in the practice room was light enough in the darkness of that concert hall.

Jesus did not begin to prepare for the cross as Pilate washed his hands, but rather when he submitted to his own washing. Last night's surrender in the Garden was just the latest in a daily submission of heart and mind. Even in that Friday darkness the light within could not be extinguished.

The end of another Lenten journey approaches. Jesus rides from Hosanna through Gethsemane to Ecce Homo. He will not bend the knee to the secular or religious principalities and powers to save himself. He offers God's light to the world, a light he carries within.

We were never promised that God's light would overcome the darkness. We are promised that the light shines in the darkness and that the darkness will not overcome it. The darkness and the light continue all the while. That Good Friday light continues to shine in and through the ones who have been handed the torch. In peace, we offer God's light to the world, not as a solution, but as another way.

UNFINISHED

We live in a small cottage surrounded by woods. For many years it only had a few weeks of summer use so we could get by with just a basic shell. We became accustomed to looking at craft-faced insulation wall covering. Some of the bare plywood floors were painted and some revealed their tree origins. For twenty years a picnic table in the kitchen served for breakfast, lunch and dinner. A clear plastic vapor barrier kept the insulation in the high ceiling. The place gave us much and demanded little.

A few years ago the time came for us to move in and live full time. We needed many things: interior walls, ceilings, stairs, door and window trim, as well as floor covering over the bare plywood. Our carpenter Bob did a wonderful job for us. He worked like he was the one who would be living in the house. All that Bob could do for us he did. The work-vacuum made the final pass over the floor and all his tools were transferred to the Ford pickup. Bob shakes our hands, smiles and says, "It's all finished." We glance at each other as he takes his leave and the Ford disappears up the driveway. After all we have been through together he has become like family.

Now it is our turn. There is more bare wood and sheetrock than I care to notice waiting to be finished: moldings, pickets, baseboards, doors, doorframes, sashes and sills. It will only be finished when we get out the brushes, drop cloth, ladder, and transfer finish from can to wood and wall. Since I find painting to be among the most tedious tasks assigned by our banishment from Eden, I am highly creative at finding excuses to postpone. But, try as I may, the bare wood says "good morning" to me as I transfer from horizontal to vertical and the bare doors say "good night" as I board the train to another country.

"It is finished" are the last words that St. John remembers Jesus speaking from the cross.[12] I have been wondering to whom Jesus was speaking as he said this. Were the words directed to Abba? Was he speaking to the few family and friends courageous enough to come all the way to Golgotha? Was it to the thieves? Was Jesus talking to himself, a self-benediction that he had accomplished all he had set out to do? Sometimes we talk to ourselves because no one else seems interested in what we say.

The Christian Church hears "It is finished" as a word of triumph. We have proclaimed to the world that these are the words of a man who has kept the faith. They are the words of a runner crossing the finish line and breaking the tape just before being escorted to the winner's circle. This is central dais, gold metal, laurel wreath, and national anthem.

The last word from the cross, according to St. John, is a word of completion. Jesus' final word was not a word to himself, not to God, and not to his mother and friends. "It is finished'" is a word for the whole church, his entire family of disciples. It is a word for all those who labor on the Easter side of the cross. It is the word of completion that empowers commencement.

I have promised myself that this summer I will stain and polyurethane the wood. Cross my heart! I sit in the living room, I look around at thirsty pine and I swear it speaks to me. There is a lot to do and it is a bit daunting to be sure. On the other hand, by imagination I can see how much more lovely our home will be wearing a new satin-gloss coat.

I have reached the place in my life when I think more about finishing than starting. I think about what I intended to accomplish on my walk and how many miles remain. I think about what I want to complete before casting crowns. I think about what I will leave the family that adopted me at my baptism. I remember all that I have received in this household. I reflect upon what I have returned.

A faithful congregation has gone before us. Countless, nameless saints across the ages have taken up their cross, carried it life-long to finish their course in faith and have won their rest. As they set their burdens down, others have been there to hoist them and set out on the next leg of the journey. They have carried us from there to here. Somewhere along the way I became aware that I was carrying something as well. It may be a cross or perhaps a backpack. It may just be a shopping bag. It any case it is mine to carry.

The pine trim and primed sheetrock have become a metaphor for much. Unfinished work calls my name. I have a lot of the practical work of discipleship to complete: compassion, charity, outreach, witness, and gratitude, to name a few. I am still a work in progress, a soul under construction, and a practical divinity in waiting. Some days I stumble forward. Other days I just stumble.

He says to us, "It is finished." And we know that it is because he finished what he came to do that we are empowered to finish what we are given to do. He seems to be asking that we redeem the time to help make it possible for others to hear the promise of the life abundant. He invites us to be his family in time and in eternity. He introduces himself all the while wearing a thousand disguises.

Bob drives the red Ford off to what is the next unfinished for him. The fragrance of polyurethane becomes incense of the unfinished for me: wood to seal and promises to keep.

THREE DAYS

There is nothing quite like the approach of Easter to summon my wandering spirit home. There is no other week in the year like the one we call "Holy." For the members of our tribe all of the great issues of salvation history come into focus in the span of a few days. It is the season when the prodigals receive another invitation to a meal of home-cooked soul food.

We begin with a parade where even stones have enough common sense to shout the truth. It all seemed clear enough on that carnival morning while we laughed through our alleluias. Too soon, however, the scene shifts: reluctantly washed feet, a Seder with a twist, the kiss of death, friends falling over one another in abandonment, the lash on an innocent back, political dereliction, suffocation by cross and hasty burial in a charity grave. It is the Friday we call "good." The sweep of it all takes the breath away and leaves us numb. If we have courage enough to remain with the women and keep their lonely vigil, we might hear God weeping.

By Saturday evening, if we have been paying attention, the hosannas have circled back to laugh in our face. The bread is stale and the wine sour. Grief suppresses the appetite in any case. The government is out to make an example of those who will not bend the knee before Caesar and, perhaps, even those who will. Knowing that the next knock on the door may be someone who wants to kiss us, fear drives us underground. Doors are locked and voices lowered. The light is taken down from the lamp stand and hidden under a bushel. What was done to him can all the more easily be done to us. We have exhausted our store of salt.

It is a drama played on an ancient stage, in a far-away land, in a language we cannot speak, and with a cast of unknowns, although there are some who appear vaguely familiar. That moment of awareness is profoundly disquieting, however. It is better to avert the eyes. You never know whom you might recognize in that crowd.

At the start of the new week grief is confounded by a story too good to be true. The mystery of Easter is as deep and profound as that of Friday. It is certainly not that Sunday trumps Friday. If anything, one merely deepens the mystery of the other. Easter gives Good Friday its meaning and Good Friday returns the favor: *Sine qua non.* The Church provides the Paschal Triduum, Maundy Thursday to Easter, to ponder wondrous love. We walk a balance beam of competing emotions; hope and common sense war within.

There is little fruit or comfort in trying to unravel the mystery at the end of that one week and the beginning of the next. Some debate the specific geography of the cross and tomb. Some insist that one particular understanding of death and resurrection is the secret handshake permitting admission to the Body. Some chase after laboratory findings on the Shroud of Turin in hope that science will guarantee what faith has not. We are still the Jews demanding signs and the Greeks lusting after wisdom that St. Paul named in Corinth.

If Friday and Sunday were stripped of mystery, they would likewise be stripped of power. Better to live the wonder of atonement and resurrection than to take one's rest in archaeology, blood tests, and carbon dating. Science is a valued partner in this dance, but it can only take us to the door of faith. We must enter alone.

Easter after all is more a matter of the heart than of the mind. Easter is more a matter of the heart than the eyes. Our heart knows things that our mind cannot understand. Our heart understands things that our eyes cannot see.

We are finally left to bet our lives on the witness of those who said that they were there. We take their word for it or we do not. We embrace their testimony and stand in amazement that whatever they experienced that weekend long ago empowered them to claim the world for its truth. That story is still food and drink in our wilderness. Within that story we recognize our face in the crowd.

Resurrection becomes a reality for us as the Good Friday-Easter truth of our baptism claims us. Holy Week reminds us that what was done time-out-of-mind is still being done every day. We are blessed to see what is hidden from our eyes. We are possessed by what our mind cannot comprehend. A holy foolishness invites us to dance. It is a story too good not to be true.

EASTER

RESURRECTION

How long had it been since they first heard the knock at the door– days or weeks? Time escapes remembering when you can taste your fear. They do not answer the door. They know who it is. They know what he wants. If they ignore the stranger, perhaps he will go away. But the knocking persists and the door begins to give way. They take turns at the door, blocking it with their backs and shoulders.

At last, when they know that the caller will soon have his way in this house, they send an urgent message to their friend. A neighbor carries the plea, "Please come quickly, your friend is deathly ill." The plea is a prayer: come by here.[1]

But their last best hope of heaven and earth does not appear. We understand that a doctor or a priest or a policeman might not come immediately. They have others in their care, and we need to wait our turn. But we expect much more from a friend.

The door gives way and the unwelcome visitor makes his grim entry to issue the summons no one refuses. The door now stands open. Who locks the house after the thief has come? The sisters learn the dull ache of a wound which does not bleed or heal. They go through the motions of what must be done, knowing a hunger that no funeral food can satisfy. They shuffle in a grief-drunk haze.

The one for whom they had prayed finally arrives. But even before he can lay his hand to the front gate she runs out to confront him. The few words that escape carry pain, frustration, disappointment, anger, and accusation. "If you had been here, my brother would not have died." She speaks for every one of us who has placed our shoulder against that door and waited for the knocking to stop. We forgive her in the instant because she carries water for the rest of us. We know what it is like to wait for a rescue that does not come.

The one lately to arrive does not defend himself. He makes no excuse. He offers no explanation. He speaks no condolence. He tells the grieving sister that her brother's future will not be what it appears to be right now.

63

In a long ago and far away place, on a dusty road well-watered with tears, he speaks to her. They are words that frame her future, as well as the future of a dead brother, now wrapped in grave-clothes and beginning to stink to high heaven. The words are for every one of us who has stood ankle deep in tear-stained dust and ashes, wrapped in our own frail arms.

"You don't have to wait for the end. I am, right now, resurrection and life. The one who believes in me, even though he or she dies, will live. And everyone who lives believing in me does not ultimately die at all. Do you believe this?"

Now there is a question the answer upon which you stake your life. He doesn't offer the woman a book, a philosophical treatise, an argument, a journal article, a ticket to a lecture, or an invitation to a small group meeting. He offers her a promise wrapped up in a person. Here I am, he says, I am here for you and for everyone who will take my word for it. I am the one who has come to give you permission to open the door when that knock comes. I am the one who holds the royal flush when the final cards are shown. I offer you resurrection and life, not someday but right now, not somewhere but right here, not just today but forever.

And, God bless her, in one of the most grace-filled moments in recorded time, she says for herself and all of us anchored in the dust of our own lives, "I believe that you are the promised one God sent to save us."

There were two miracles in Bethany that day. The first miracle is that Lazarus is called forth from the stench, unbound and freed. In many ways it is the lesser miracle because he is only returned to his family for a little while. He must re-enter that tomb once again.

But there was also that other miracle. It is the miracle when the grieving woman receives the grace to see with the eyes of faith; when she embraces God's promise of resurrection. She is one of our mothers in the faith. Life eternal is to know God's love in the one who arrives too late for the funeral but at the right time for the resurrection.

We soon meet Mary again in John's Gospel.[2] Mary, Martha, and Lazarus gather for a dinner with Jesus when she takes herself off to a secret place and returns with a pound of liquid gold. The contents of that jar are her life's savings, a year's wages. And before God and all the people she literally lets her hair down, pours that sweet perfume on the feet of the one she loves, and wipes his feet with her hair: treasure, hair, perfume and a beauty to break the heart. The scent of the oil would sweeten the air in that house for a long, long time. The next day Jesus climbs upon the back of a donkey and rides into Jerusalem, the sweet fragrance trailing behind.

She gives her earthly treasure to anoint his feet in this public proclamation because of what he has already given her. She received her brother back for a while; yes, of course. But the greater gift was that she knew in that holy encounter she had entered into the life eternal, she had taken hold of the gracious gift of another kind of future. She could see her whole life the way you view the ocean from the shore. She said "yes", and in that leap of faith her future changed. In that "yes", futures change.

Let the knock come. Her future was God. Let the knock come. We know who is on the other side of the door.

FLYING LESSON

I really believed that I would be able to fly. Much of that belief was grounded in the rich fantasy life of a fourth-grader, a boy steeped in one comic book hero who was a "strange visitor from another planet" who soared in the cause of "truth, justice and the American way" and another, a Saturday matinee serial wonder, who slipped on a rocket parka before leaping skyward to the rescue. At a deeper level, it was merely the willing suspension of disbelief.

Some neighborhood pals and I discovered several curious, pneumatic vests in one of the family garages. My friends, older and wiser, convinced me that they were flying vests. If you strapped one on and inflated it by blowing into an attached rubber tube, you would be able to take flight. There was sufficient mystery about the arcane vests, as well as my own desire to ascend on eagle's wings, that I was eager to try. We agreed to return to the garage after dark, don our vests, and rise together into the night sky. At the appointed hour, we secreted the vests from the garage and headed out to the hill behind the cemetery. Following the lead of my companions, we climbed to the summit, inflated the flying vests, and prepared for take-off.

Since I was the only one in this seminar who had never used a flying vest before, they elected me to solo first. The flight instructions were simple: run down the hill as fast as you can, extend your arms like wings, and just before you reach the bottom, the flight vest will give you the power to take off. They instructed me not to go too high the first time. Get some experience before you try anything acrobatic. In order to land gracefully, they instructed me to pull the air release cord and gradually return to earth.

Call me Clark Kent. Down the grassy hill with the confidence of a true believer, I ran as fast as my nine-year-old legs would carry me, arms fully extended, waiting to be carried aloft to the dazzling wonders of the night sky. By the time I got to the bottom of the hill, however, I began to suspect that something was wrong. Not only was I not soaring with the eagles but I was also hearing an unwelcome sound from the top of the hill. What began as giggles quickly turned into howls of laughter. Willing suspension of disbelief evaporated in a moment of childhood clarity. I sheepishly re-made the summit to the sound of their hilarity and wisecracks. Call me Clark Gullible.

It was an early experience of gotcha. What was too good to be true was in fact. I had believed the wrong people: a small step on the road to maturity and no real harm done. It has not been my only experience of misplaced trust, which for most of us is a continuing education course with many fellow students. People sometimes tell you things that you believe to be true but which subsequently turn out to be false. It is not necessarily a justification for cynicism, but deception can mightily disappoint, even break our hearts. It is a tale told east of Eden, an experience recapitulated often along the way. If it were otherwise, humans would be something other than what we are. We forgive even as we ask for forgiveness. Class is continually in session.

What we believe is generally a consequence of the ones we believe. Our trust of the source opens the door to trusting the message. Those who do not have our trust do not often have their word taken at face value. The road to trust is paved with reliability.

According to St. John, at one point in Jesus' ministry, the teacher was being pursued and pestered about his identity. Once again, they wanted to know if he was the one who had been promised of old. We can hear him sigh across the centuries as he makes his exasperated reply, "I told you, and you do not believe…because you do not belong to my sheep".[3] They do not know him so they will not believe him. They are not even able to believe the evidence of their own eyes and ears.

In matters of faith, we believe on someone else's word. Often we have nowhere else to go. We were not there, not that it would make much difference if we were. We know from our own experience that just because we see it does not mean that we shall believe. There is no reliable scientific test for evidence known only in the heart, an assurance of things not seen. The more important something is, the more impossible it is to prove. When absolute certainty is required, faith translates the conversation and speaks another language. Only the sheep who belong to the fold know their shepherd, follow where their shepherd leads and believe what their shepherd says.

In the life and death matters of faith, it always comes down to the same question: what shepherd do you follow? That decision, once made, opens our ears to the voice that offers the way, the truth, and the life. It is food for our deepest hunger, an answer to the prayer too deep for words, and flying instructions to get us up off the ground.

LOCKED

Reality returns. The flowers are gone, just a trace of their fragrance lingers in the deserted sanctuary. Bright hues are muted. Some fugitive bulletins, memorial flower lists, peppermint candy wrappers, and special offering envelopes are littered among the pews. Risen-today-anthems are returned to the file cabinet in the music room. The ensemble of Easter and Christmas mavericks has dispersed to more familiar Sabbath routines: sleeping in, robes, bagels, third cups of coffee and a kilo of Sunday Times. Each has its particular charm.

We sometimes wonder what the Christmas and Easter folk make of what we are doing at worship. If you only come twice a year, only at full-house celebrations, you might think that worship consists of triumphant singing and hothouse flowers. Birth and resurrection are not bad news, of course, but not a full gospel either.

Every church has at least two congregations. One meets week after week, year round, in season and out. Another gathers semi-annually when the wider culture parallels our celebrations with homage to a North Pole saint and a rabbit. We can count on folks to know when to show up for a good time, although we can hardly blame them for that. We live in the hope that the first congregation will get larger and the second smaller.

We try not to judge the bi-annual folks. We announce that we have thrown open our hearts, minds and doors. We will leave a light on for you. You never know, a seed scattered here and there. In any case, the quality of a person's character is not measured by Sabbath observance. We would not want our character measured only by what we do in weekly installments with the like-minded. It is best to leave all those judgments in more gracious hands.

If you don't return the week after Easter, however, you will miss the rest of the story. St. John reminds us that there were two parts to Easter: morning and evening. The first light brings the discovery by three breathless disciples of a displaced stone, an empty charnel house and a case of mistaken identity.[4] We sing a happy morning anthem; risen today. We own that song like no other; alleluia.

Easter evening is another matter entirely.[5] The Gospel text reminds us that you can believe that Jesus is risen and still hide behind locked doors. It is the day of resurrection but the sun has not set before joy and hope have taken their leave. If the authorities can kill the teacher, what will they do to the students? If we dare to stand with them in our imagination, we are likewise double-checking the dead bolts.

Doors get locked because we are afraid. There is a growth industry just now that promises to help us dwell secure by means of all manner of sophisticated locks and alarms. In theory, at least, we are more secure locked in and others locked out. We would be foolish to ignore prudent protection: lock in and lock out, lock up and lock down. We have Kryptonite for the bike and a direct line to the police for the bedroom. The good shepherd comes with a security camera and silent alarm.

But other doors get locked too. We secure the doors of our hearts and minds against those who are different from us. Fear locks the door and hangs out the *cave canem*. Hospitality is suppressed, suspicion multiplied and reasons reinforced. No foreigners, heretics, law-breakers, enemies, sinners, unbelievers, misfits, or apostates need knock. If I let them into my life, there is no telling how God might ask me to change.

Locked door no obstacle, Jesus comes and stands among his own to reclaim and restore those who ran away, those who denied, those who deserted, those who could not stay awake, and those complicit in crucifixion. He would have reclaimed the one who betrayed him if he were there. "Peace be with you." He breathes on them. They inhale and learn there is more to life than air alone: a matter of breath and life. There is nothing to keep Jesus from those he loves, nothing to silence his healing word, and nothing to prevent the free flow of his breath of new life.

The real work of Easter does not begin in the morning light of hyacinth-fragrant sanctuaries, lovely as they are, but rather in the dusk of stuffy, locked rooms. Easter always begins where we live, too often out of shalom, a day late and a dollar short, and struggling to catch our breath. Easter begins when God is experienced in the midst of our fear, our anger, our loneliness, our obsession, our arrogance and our misplaced priorities: standing within the shadow of our own mortality.

Easter begins to happen when God's shalom–God's forgiveness–God's persistence–God's breath–unlocks all our fearful doors. We open our eyes and discover that He is already standing among us. He enters without even knocking.

In memory of William W. Reid, Jr.

PENTECOST

PLAYING WITH FIRE

I did a double take. I was sure that my eyes were having me on. It has happened before, of course. It could just be a variation on the mistaken identity that regularly inflicts aging eyes. Settling back into the cushioned pulpit furniture after the processional, I was strategically positioned to get an unobstructed view of the back of the pulpit. Being an occasional visitor to chancels, I get to see the preacher-side of pulpits now and again. This time I looked once, twice, three times. This was a new one on me.

Can you tell anything about a church from what is stored in the pulpit? Of course, there are those that have a hinged door to keep the contents out of sight. In those cases, I am just left to wonder what is behind the door as the last notes of the prelude fade and the call to worship reclaims me. There is nothing systematic about my observations, you understand, it is just a curiosity that takes possession of my attention until I get around to the next order of business. Some congregations use the pulpit cavity as the community lost and found, the church history repository, or the supply closet.

I have seen pulpits that were packed so full that I had to hold my water glass for want of a few inches resting place. I recall Bibles in every version since the Latin Vulgate, hymnals representing every division and merger of the denomination for 200 years, bulletins for advent 1979, burned stumps of candles in any liturgical color you care to name, assorted flower vases for birth buds or funeral bouquets, match books from the Golden Nugget, nubs of pew pencils with broken points, dusty glass communion cups, brocade Bible markers for Pentecost, books of children's Bible stories, a reminder to someone "don't forget the offering", printed heartfelt prayer requests for friends and loved ones, reading glasses in several strengths, assorted microphone cords and spare batteries, and a final page from a sermon that never traveled to the next service.

Sure enough, upon closer scrutiny, my first impression was accurate: it was a fire extinguisher. My mind went wandering off into a flight of fancy as to the reason for a fire extinguisher in the pulpit.

Perhaps the folks thought that if a fire broke out the preacher could see it first and react to it right away. The pulpit was essentially empty except for that piece of emergency equipment. Someone clearly wanted it there for a reason. Tall, red, and sporting a tag indicating that it had been recently inspected, it was ready for action.

Driving to my next stop, I was kidnapped by that fire extinguisher. The more I thought about it, the more I felt that having a fire extinguisher pulpit-side could well be understood as a statement of faith about what can happen in worship. Perhaps the fire extinguisher should be regularly and prominently placed upon the communion table for all to see. Let it be a reminder of the Holy Fire upon whom we call in our prayers.

Our prayers of invocation are intoned sleepily, casually and perfunctorily. We plead with the Spirit of God to come upon us and set us aflame with a passion for God. We beg for an infusion of transforming power to set our hearts on fire. We invite the divine presence to "come by here," "fall afresh on us," and "our hearts inspire." The extinguisher might serve to remind us that we are playing with fire when we keep issuing such invitations to God. Jesus said that he "came to bring fire to the earth and I wish it were already kindled!"[1]

One of these days, our blithe prayers might just get answered in full view of pastor, choir and congregation. If that Pentecost fire does come calling some walls will be pushed out, some doors removed from their hinges and the roof raised. The order of worship will be set aside that Sunday as some things are re-ordered. The word "awesome" will recover some of its original meaning.

Not such a bad idea to keep that red canister out in full view for all to see. Admittedly, it is a peculiar icon for most of our sanctuaries. However, it is an appropriate symbol for an alert and expectant people, for those that stand on tiptoe, and for those in an advent state of mind. We should be playing with fire. Who can say when our prayers will be answered? For all of that, when the fire comes calling, the extinguisher will be of no consequence.

UNWILLING

I have never possessed a particularly warm and fuzzy feeling for Methodist father-in-faith, John Wesley. I have tremendous respect and admiration for him, you understand. It is just that his single-minded discipleship, his discipline, his ability to will one thing and his callous disregard of his own comfort have all kept me at arm's length, as it were. Iron John was a visionary genius who mobilized a movement of scriptural Christianity to transform a nation. Thank God and Amen! If he stood in another faith tradition, his canonization would be assured. If he were my supervisor, I might hope to serve in another district.

I do not deny any of my long-standing admiration. However, there is at least one place in his life where I get a glimpse of an honest-to-God human being. In a life that spanned virtually the entire 18th century, there is one moment when I feel a deeper bond of kinship to John Wesley than all his sermons preached, all his miles in the saddle, and his the societies, classes and bands broadcast by his organizational inspiration.

That occasion was the night of his conversion. The story is well known in Wesley lore. He had been agitated in spirit for days, coming off a failure in Georgia, recently inspired by his contact with the Moravians, and desperately hungry for an inner peace that would set a troubled heart to rest. On that day in May 1738, he recalled later in his journal, he had been led to believe that he was standing on the strand of an epiphany. He remembers that he went to a prayer meeting at a home on Aldersgate Street and in the course of that service, through intermediaries St. Paul, Martin Luther, and the Holy Spirit, he was claimed by the inner assurance for which he hungered. He would never be the same again. "A slave redeemed from death and sin/a brand plucked from eternal fire."[2] He became a spark that ignited a movement whose glow warms us even now.

What is so powerful for me about that evening is not the conversion itself, moving as that account is. What claims me is that John Wesley did not want to go to that prayer meeting.[3] We do not know why. Perhaps he had enough church for one day. Perhaps he was tired, having begun his Bible study at 5 AM. Perhaps he wanted to remove his boots, put his feet up, and relax. Perhaps there was someone there he did not want to see. In any case, he writes that he went to Aldersgate Street "very unwillingly." I may love him as much for those two words as for the entirety of his legacy. Beneath his exemplary and formidable discipleship, there is a glimpse of humanity and vulnerability that lets me in.

There is more of my discipleship than I care to admit when I drag myself to Aldersgate Street. As much as not, I take myself to where I need to go rather than where I want to go. Duty trumps desire. Some of this is just because I am an introvert who does not easily seek out the unknown. Truth to be told, virtually all of the life-changing events and people of my life were encountered after some reluctance was overcome. Unwillingness names me. It may in part be introversion. It may be just one more personal imperfection. I wish that I had more spontaneous enthusiasm and delight in the opportunities before me day by day. But if that were the case, I would be someone else.

What continues to amaze me is that the people and places where my reluctance has been greatest have often turned out to be the very ones that held the most significant change, growth, maturity, learning, and transformation. I am learning to pay closer attention to where I do not want to go. The dominical admonition is toward narrow gates and hard roads. Reluctance overcome has been a map to travel a road that would not otherwise be taken.

Aldersgate, where a very unwilling Wesley was graced with his heart's desire, may well be the name of every way where transformation awaits the reluctant traveler.

REDEEMED ATTENTION

For reasons known only to providence, I was not present at the distribution of the artistic gifts. While I love fine art, taking regular opportunities to visit museums, galleries and studios, I myself am unable to draw more than the proverbial "flies." My development as an artist was arrested somewhere in elementary school. Even now as I try to place on paper what my eye can see, it appears the doodles of a child. The mystic harmony between eye, mind and hand eludes me. I covet the artistic gift and have deep admiration for those who can express themselves with brush and paint. I also know that if I had been given that gift I would be someone else.

I have a friend who is an artist. She is as excellent an artist as she is a person and I delight to her art and to her wisdom. She sees things I cannot see. She looks at rocks and trees and skies and seas and notes a depth of beauty of which I am unaware. Her paintings offer an ensemble of rocks, shells, flowers and feathers in a wondrous delight for sore eye and heart. She collects rocks. I ban rocks from my garden. The difference between us is that she can look at a rock and discern an inner truth about that particular rock. All rocks appear the same to me. Betty patiently waits in the presence of a rock for it to reveal itself. I assume that a rock's only value is what it can do for me or against me. She can name rocks that to me are anonymous. When she learns their names they sometimes appear in her paintings. I am not able to paint what I cannot name.

When I ask Betty about the inner life of rocks and shells and flowers and feathers, she says that it is a matter of "paying attention." And I suspect that is the difference between us. What reveals itself to her is hidden from me by virtue of the attention paid. If I could see with Betty's eye and heart, the stones would begin to shout.

What came to mind after one conversation with Betty was a comment by Simone Weil about prayer. Weil wrote that at its root prayer was a matter of paying attention.[4] Her word offers me an insight, a means and a challenge. To look but not see, to listen but not hear, to eat but not taste, to be in the presence but not to be present are all matters of paying attention. It is why we are well advised to enter a quiet room, close the door, close the eyes, clear the mind and then turn our attention God-ward. What at first is hidden may then begin to reveal itself.

It is a truth about the life of relationship as well. To pay attention to another human being is to open the possibility of learning what appears to be hidden. When St. Paul speaks of not regarding anyone from a human point of view any longer, he is inviting us to a redeemed attention.[5] To look at another human "in Christ" is to see a life both whole and holy. In one other person reverently encountered there is a salvation story waiting to be heard. It is grace to learn the names of those who are anonymous to the world. It is grace to learn our own names in the holy attention of someone else.

Our electronic culture has done us few favors. There are no sound bites which can reveal another's heart and soul. The culture of mass media educates for the superficial, immediate, and manageable. Don't ponder; react. Don't inquire; take someone's word for it. Don't reflect; accept. A blizzard of images snows us and then quickly moves on before we can name the truth. We are well informed but we know very little. The media plugs into us and we are distracted and anesthetized. If we were to pay attention, it would be endangered. We do not necessarily need to eliminate but we do need to pay attention.

In clear contrast are all those like my friend Betty who sits attentively before nature until it reveals a truth to her. In clear contrast are those who understand what it means to no longer regard others from a human point of view. In clear contrast are those who are attentive before God, waiting to learn what only prayer can reveal.

In honor of Betty Bryden

ORDINARY TIME

ALL IN THE FAMILY

THE COMPANY WE KEEP

As a way to supplement income from the sale of summer-bounty tomatoes, beans and squash, the Amish farmer constructed a variety of handmade, wooden, garden and porch items. They were well made, attractive and priced fairly enough to have wide appeal. He would sell the items wholesale to dealers who would in turn market them. One particular dealer, however, cheated the farmer. He did not pay what he said, did not keep his end of the bargain, and refused to honor the agreement. The farmer was counseled to engage an attorney and bring legal action against the dealer to recover the financial loss. He was encouraged to at least seek simple justice and not allow himself to be cheated. The Amish craftsman refused such counsel with the words, "No, that is not our way."

A friend related the story to me from his personal experience with the farmer. We were having a conversation about what was distinctive about a Christian lifestyle. Was the farmer foolish or admirable? Are there particular, peculiar, elements of a Christian lifestyle that can be observed by the way a person lives in the world? Are there things that a Christian would consistently do, or refrain from doing, in his or her workaday world that gives clear witness to a Christian faith? If so, what might they be? Can I be Rambo one day and St. Francis the next? It is a syllabus to sustain more than one seminar.

If we are truly salt to savor the unsavory and light to scatter the shadows, then there should be some evidence that we are present. Of course, salt can lose savor and light can be concealed within a variety of containers. The Sunday sermon may fuel our heartfelt longing to love one another as we have been loved, but then we must inevitably confront someone who cheats us. A kind of amnesia can occur between the benediction and the world beyond the sound of the organ postlude. I am far more proficient at paying homage to moral sentiments than acting upon them.

One thing that struck me about the Amish farmer's reply to his counselors was his use of the word "our", as in "our way." Owing his Christian identity in large measure to the community that formed and sustained him, he was not facing the cheater alone. He was not just an

83

individual Christian believer. He belonged to a people with an identity defined for life in the world. He came to the dilemma of the crooked dealer with a deeply ingrained understanding so that the way he responded was not his own ego-sense of justice, fair play, revenge, or pay back. He was accountable to his entire community for the way he responded to being cheated. Legal action was not one option among the several. I suspect that he did not need to consider his response. I imagine that, if God had granted me the grace to respond in a similar way, I most likely would have said, "No, it's not my way."

My sense of community is generally so attenuated as scarcely to allow the use of the word. I am a creature of a very heterogeneous Christian assembly. I keep company with independent rugged-individualists who do ethics largely out of a God-and-me mixture of selective Biblical memory, folk wisdom, frontier justice and prevailing cultural norms. I am a Christian citizen who can't remember if I belong to Romans 13 or Revelation 13 or both. I am a church member caught between demanding Biblical norms on the one hand and sound business practices on the other. I am a disciple who has largely managed to mollify the hard sayings of Jesus into a comfortable, pragmatic, personal religiosity.

It can be a lonely pilgrimage to be accountable principally to conscience. I find myself coveting the Amish farmer's clarity at the ethical crossroads. There are, no doubt, drawbacks to a community of such homogeneity, conformity and intensity. I know well that it demands a life to which I am not suited by either birth or temperament. I would not, however, deny that more clarity and security would attend to "our way." I would welcome more fellow travelers at the crossroads, companions in the dilemmas.

Many of us have more church than we want and less community than we need. I believe that the deeper hunger within us is for the latter more than the former. It is in Christian community where ethical clarity can begin to occur, in community where my beliefs and actions can be tested and held to account, and in community where I can begin to both learn and live my true identity.

The company we keep also keeps us. The grace we experience in community can gradually transform "my way" into "our way."

UNNATURAL ACTS

I t is a standing mystery why some things I hear or read stick to my brain as if they were written on flypaper while others slide off as if scratched on Teflon. Typically the sticking and the sliding are in a perverse correlation with my need or desire to remember. In my case, the slippery things I would truly love to retain include the names of the twelve Apostles, the Seven Deadly Sins, the spelling of Habakkuk, and my cell phone number. Unfortunately, what does adhere are wisecrack one-liners by Mel Brooks, the secret words to keep Gort from destroying the world in *The Day the Earth Stood Still*, and the tire pressure for my first bicycle. Synapses have a mischievous life of their own.

Waiting for a lesson in my piano teacher's living room, reading the jokes in a coffee table issue of *Readers Digest*, I stumbled upon an article with the approximate title, "The Pleasure of Doing Good Secretly." The author went on about the joy of performing good deeds anonymously. Do the deed, he gushed, and then stand back and watch from behind the curtain, smiling inwardly at your little conspiracy while the recipient ponders the identity of his or her benefactor. It was an earlier version of practice acts of "random kindness." All this was a few minutes one Saturday afternoon more than a half-century ago. In any case, the article was printed on contact paper.

Re-surfacing from some subterranean archive, it comes visiting a half-century later as I am reading Matthew 6. Jesus instructs his disciples about a higher righteousness that includes, among other things, his teaching regarding revenge, anger, lust, divorce, forgiveness and enemies. He then proceeds to meddle further with our comfortable piety by denying us the pleasure of getting what we think we deserve from our generosity. He says, "But when you give alms, do not let your left hand know what your right hand is doing, so that your alms may be done in secret; and your Father who sees in secret will reward you."[1] We can't get even, we can't indulge our anger, lust, or hate and now we can't bask in the neighbors' admiration of our beneficence.

As far as I can tell, Jesus had two basic things to say about our attitude toward our possessions. He urged both that we give generously on the one hand and anonymously on the other. They are both challenging and, on any given day, equally so. They are two sides of the same coin, as it were. As we should come to expect by now, his admonition flies squarely in the face of all of our natural inclinations. This is no surprise because Matthew 6 has all along been telling us things that we do not want to hear. The chapter is an unrelenting list of unnatural acts.

It is an ethic for the Kingdom of God, of course, an ethic of excess, reflecting the prodigality of God.[2] Give as God gives, good measure pressed down running over on the one hand and secretly on the other. It is as rigorous a test of our going-on-to-perfection as any.

Surprised by occasional moments of interior candor, I wonder if I really trust that God will notice my giving and record it in the appropriate celestial ledger. I seem to prefer basking in my neighbor's appreciation here and now rather than risk God's failure to notice and reward later. I want to hedge my bets and take my testimonial dinner in full view of the largest audience I can assemble in utter humility. It is no great stretch for me to imagine that the same word applies to my time and talent as well as my treasure. I want assurance that my service will be as noticed, praised and appreciated as my largess. My checkbook and calendar stand at mute attention awaiting conversion.

Admittedly, it is radical giving: generously and secretly. At root such discipleship asks me to take Jesus at his word that God knows what I need and will provide it. If I really trusted that promise, it would make me ready to give in such a way that it would be known only to God. It might make me ready to give it all away. I could give it away because, in God's economy, there is always more where that came from.

I guess there was some truth in that sticky article on the coffee table that I needed to learn. It turns out to be one variation on a theme in the larger symphony of Matthew 6. Now and then I get to humming a few bars in one of my practice rooms. I am still trying to learn how to play that tune.

JIMMY

Polishing Sunday shoes, a whiff of leather and Kiwi, I become aware of him at my side. No annunciation. He is a welcome sight for the inward eye.

Transported by brush and polish to Jimmy's Shoe Repair on Mill Street in summer 1955, I am once again the free-pick-up-and-delivery-kid on my red single-speed-Columbia with deep wire basket, knocking on doors and gathering in shoes of every denomination that wanted redemption. From my canvas bag I assemble tethered pairs like a congregation on Jimmy's counter.

Two by two he transfers them to the last in the front window surgery where he and his world are in full view. Humming with an ancient radio spilling pop songs from the top shelf he ties the blue apron, wields hammer and tongs, waves to passing neighbors and chews his Black Jack. An occasional Italian expletive escapes.

Few knew that Jimmy held their soles and heels in such caring, calloused hands. He apprenticed with an orthopedic shoemaker and for that he knew uneven wear, turned-in-turned-out gait, aching ankles, and lopsided stance. He intuitively understood level and straight. He studied the shoes until correct surrendered.

By subtle amendments to leather and rubber, Jimmy fashioned a repair that urged the foot toward center and balance. No fanfare. No extra charge. It was his contribution to make the crooked straight and the rough plain.

When he was satisfied, each pair passed to me to be polished, bagged, and returned. The counter cleared, tired chestnut hands locked the shop and he headed home in the two-tone Chevy.

A scent calls him back. He watches in silence as I brush and buff for Sunday. His approval still means something to me. I breathe it in. He is out of bounds now.

Few ever knew that Jimmy was looking out for them. In his shoes we stood a little straighter. Knowing him, we walked a little more upright.

In memory of James Garzella

87

MARATHON MAN

I am a stranger here. I quickly do a first-visit scan of the room. My eye comes to rest upon a tee shirt. The size and boldness of the print declare that it is a shirt with a message intended for others. What other purpose might a printed tee shirt have? My myopia deciphers the pronouncement across the food court: Mohawk-Hudson Marathon. To judge by the low-fat physique of the wearer I am ready to believe that this is a trophy in token of successful completion of 26+ miles. The owner appears able to go the distance. The middle-aged marathoner is seated at a table with another, considerably older, person. Midday, we are all here for lunch; food court fare between meetings. It is food for the body if not the soul, a no-carb-left-behind festival.

I have the advantage of an oblique angle that allows me to observe the runner's table while presiding over my tuna on rye and diet cola, doing my best to ignore the fragrance of freshly baked cinnamon rolls. My colleagues and I have business to occupy us, but occasionally I glance across the playing field of Formica and French Fries and take note of the runner and his lunch companion.

If physical resemblance is a reliable witness, the runner is having lunch with his mother. I note that she is seated in a wheelchair drawn up close upon the table. She is colorfully and tastefully attired. She might have been dressed for Sunday worship had it not been Monday. The woman sits passively in her chair. She seems to me to be particularly passive. Another glance tells the reason. She is incapacitated in ways that the wheelchair does not reveal. The clearest sign of this is that her son is feeding her lunch.

I have seen adults feeding children. I have seen adults feeding other adults. I have fed children and adults myself. On this occasion, however, my attention is kidnapped by the way in which the son is feeding his mother. It is plain to me that she is the most important person in the world. Without the slightest trace of embarrassment, impatience, or self-consciousness, the son lifts the spoon to his mother's lips and allows her to take the food from it as she will. It is a scene of quiet grace, peace, and dignity. By some imperceptible sign from her, he knows when to load the spoon and offer it again. He gently wipes her lips.

The beauty and simplicity of that tableau is invested in my memory. I do not know that I will be able to watch one person feed another again without calling to mind this mother and son, companions in deed as well as word. I am doing my best not to be an obvious audience from my table across the court, but that feeding is poignant and beautiful poetry. Amidst the scurry and din of the setting, the anxious laughter and clang, I am captured by the extravagant tenderness of his gentle, patient gestures. The sweet smell of the ointment from an alabaster jar fills the room. I wait with mother and son through the ice cream, one spoon at a time. Her smile thanks her marathon man. The epiphany suspends time, suspends me. I surrender the moment reluctantly as I re-enter table talk and tuna.

Laying about in my mind, mother and marathon man invite themselves for a return visit, passengers on my solo ride home. On one level, it is just a particular case of the fifth commandment honored in plain sight. However, the more I entertain the memory the more I come to understand that it is not the feeding itself that claims me, but the patient, loving manner in which it is done. One can provide food or one can feed.

Mother and son at lunch exemplify what I have learned to expect of such moments of serendipitous revelation. Here is beauty and judgment mixed in proportions not to be measured. The beauty inspires awe while the judgment invites examination. The beauty invites me to look above and the judgment inspires me to look within. I call to mind some times when I believed I was feeding. I understand now, in the confessional of a late afternoon ride home, that I was merely providing food. Far too often what I have offered by way of prayers, presence, gifts, or service, has been an onerous interruption, rushed to completion, resented for its inconvenience, and offered with silent self-congratulation for my generosity: O God, I thank thee that I am not like others. I offer with one hand while the other is out of sight, fingers crossed or, more likely, clenched.

We ignite ministry with open hearts, open minds, and open doors. Ministry merely smolders when doors have peepholes and safety chains, when only one hand is extended and when the heart is withheld. Our cautious reluctance denies the possibility of the dominical good measure: pressed down, shaken together, and running over.

I expect to be visited by the marathon man and his mother some other time. A knock will come to the front door of my life and I will be offered the opportunity to feed some friend or stranger. I can imagine mother and marathon man standing in silent witness to what I learned in the food court tutorial, observing whether I finish the course in grace, whether we eat and drink together in a Eucharist of the heart.

HOME

I t was about endings and beginnings: "In our end is our beginning, in our time, infinity."[3] Intimations of what is to come reside in what is. I become more pensive as an ending with a small "e" approaches. Not wearing a tie for the last time, I drink in the familiar interstate delights on a commute the Subaru could make without me. The closer the approach of this day, the greater is my reluctance. I try to make my office look like I have never been there and load the evidence of my tenure into the trunk. I peel Charlie Brown and Emily Dickinson from the door. The spider plant needs a last drink. Then there are the controlled farewells with something in my throat. Surrendering the keys, for the first time I notice the sound of the door closing behind me. Who knows where the time goes?

I have been here before, of course. Among other things we call it itinerancy. We have all been there before, whatever we call it. Beginnings have endings embedded within them. Endings make beginnings possible. It is a universal that we Christians embrace in joyful anticipation, even if the path to that day is watered with our tears.

The question that comes to visit on this last ride is, "Where is my home? Where do I really live?" This routine seemed to be easier before. Can I receive an excuse from the office of aging? It is not only more difficult to let go of what came before, but also harder to embrace what lies ahead. Uncertainty knocks on the door. Will a Peter Principle certificate soon be arriving by special delivery? Whose call did you say you were answering?

As the turn signal clicks away for my exit ramp it occurs to me, perhaps for the first time: my home is not an address. It is not a building. It is not a telephone number. It is not my name on an appointment list. It has nothing to do with where I collect mail or return calls. It is a matter of where I feel at home. It is not where the cardboard boxes get deposited. It is where my spirit finds peace. Like so many of the other signposts we encounter on the journey, I have received an invitation to entertain a deeper truth. It is not where I live that is at issue, but rather to whom I belong.

One witness remembers that on the last night of His life, Jesus tries to prepare His friends for a future without Him. His ending was going to be a beginning. If He did not leave then the Advocate could not come. We can hear the urgency in His appeal to them even as the conspirators plotted His destruction: "Make your home in me, as I make mine in you."[4] Jesus is inviting His friends, pleading even, to let become true what is already true. He is asking them to live according to the reality to which they already belong.

The life of faith is an ongoing spiritual homecoming. It seems like we are always traveling away from our true home. We are looking for something or someone else. We are a wounded people, looking for acceptance, looking for affirmation. We are full of doubts. We suspect that we may not be welcome. We worry about our worthiness. Perhaps we are not acceptable. Our need drives us to seek life in other places. Our need pulls us away from our true home.

Coming into a relationship with God is a series of homecomings. To live in that relationship is to be at home wherever we happen to find ourselves. When we are at home life doesn't frighten us so much anymore. Even the prospect of our own ending comes to be understood as just another homecoming. We turn our face homeward because we may. The prodigal heart knows the joy of open arms, the taste of fatted calf, and a robe's warm embrace. We are oriented by the memory of welcome. God's most recent embrace is always penultimate.

Home is not where you find it. Home is not even where you find yourself. Home is when you realize that you have been found.

BUT NOT RELIGIOUS

Each one of us has our own spiritual type. Or it may be more precise to say that we are a spiritual type. I suppose that I have always known this. But like so many other truths in the hidden places, it is largely unexamined. As a result of the wondrous interplay of genetics, environment, education, and the homogenizing action of God's providence, we each respond differently to the spiritual in the everyday. When the table is spread we fill our plates with the food that satisfies.

What feeds my mind, nourishes my spirit, and gives me life can leave another person standing right beside me bored or hungry, glancing at the clock or the nearest exit. Likewise, I can be standing in the midst of a hurricane of religious ecstasy as a disinterested outsider wondering about the lunch menu. Others can be passing the serpents around and I am checking to see if I have my snakebite kit. It has nothing to do with respecting the spirituality of others, which I surely do. It is just that what feeds others may not feed me. I do work to stretch my boundaries. At the great potluck meal of the family of God, it is good to sample a new casserole occasionally.

My spirituality leads me in the direction of silence, meditation, listening, Eucharist, poetry, parable, paradox, and mystery. I prefer solitude to small group conversation. I prefer listening to talking. I prefer invitation to instruction. I prefer Psalms to Leviticus. I prefer less to more. There is a part of me that instinctively shrinks from a Mardi Gras of what is most precious.

On my walk I have been claimed by questions more than answers. Questions move me to seek, pray, wonder and search. Answers, while not unwelcome, tend to curtail the expedition. When the proverbial two roads diverge in a wood, the "one less traveled by" is the one that does not end at answers but rather deepens the questions. Both roads can and do bring faithful pilgrims to their hearts' delight, no doubt. But there are at least two roads because there are at least two ways to the center. God meets us where we are and leads each of us on a path to the fullness of grace. The hunger and the food are grace from the same source.

Spirituality, like an iceberg, is more hidden than revealed. But, on the other hand, I have always believed that spirituality reveals itself in discipleship. If I never move from the silence, and if I never do anything with the parable, then my spirituality is incomplete. If I leave the cathedral unchanged I am just another tourist. And so it is a puzzle to me to know what to make of the current popular expression, "I am spiritual, but I am not religious."

In part I take the comment as a negative judgment on religion as something that is of less value than spirituality. Spiritual is something pure while religion is something messy. Spiritual makes for serenity while religion makes for strife. Spiritual gives me something while religion demands something of me. Spiritual is private while religion is public. Spiritual is of heaven while religion is of earth.

Yet, I cannot understand how being spiritual can be an end in itself. I believe that being spiritual is being present to God so we might in turn be present for others. It is a movement to the center so we might in turn move to the margins. It is the experience of the peace of God, too good not to be shared. In and of itself, spirituality can become aesthetics, beautiful sunsets to help us get to sleep, sweet music to help us forget our troubles or a retreat into me and mine. Being spiritual is wonderful, but not the whole story.

I understand that spirituality is what is happening to me in the presence of transforming grace, gradually being claimed by the life abundant. I understand religion to be sharing the Bread of Life, being present for others, moving to the margins, and pointing others to amazing grace.

And so I am puzzled about being spiritual but not religious. But in the end I am grateful when I hear it because it invites me to remember that my spirituality and my religion are just one dwelling. One is the foundation and the other the house built upon it.

ROSARY

I t was the first time in my life that I lived away from home. My childhood, adolescence and young adulthood were lived in one town. I am of one culture, one home, one school, one church and one values set. I traveled to North Carolina, a far country for a Pennsylvania boy in the early 1960's, to begin theological studies; the first of my Annual Conference clan to matriculate at this school. Family and friends wondered why I had to go so far away. Not a maverick by nature, it was a season of high anxiety to solo where no one had gone before. Amendment by addition, deletion, and substitution became my orders of the day.

New also was the experience of dormitory living and sharing a room with another human. The residence hall czars rolled the dice and placed me with Clark. He was in a graduate studies program in contemporary theology, having already completed his first degree in theology at Harvard. He was an ordained Moravian minister, transplanted from Utica, New York. He worked as a Chaplain and Instructor at a Moravian academy for women in North Carolina. We were both new to this place, strangers here, without family or friends. Clark reminded me with a smile that, if it were not that John Wesley had encountered some Moravians shipboard, there probably would not be Methodists.

It took me only a short time to realize that it was my great good fortune, blessing, to room with Clark in the Men's Graduate Center. For one thing, he knew why he was in school, knew how to study, knew how to think critically, knew how to reflect on his experience theologically, and knew how to balance his life between work and leisure. Disciplined in personal and academic habits, one of his mantras was "moderation in all things." He was wise in ways in which I was immature. He was the older brother I never had –mentor, spiritual guide and friend. He liked to laugh. He was a delight.

Clark introduced me to southern cuisine: collards, okra, hush puppies, grits, and universal pork fat. He initiated me into southern verbal expressions, the courtesies of casual interactions and the gentle grace of everyday life. We sat together in daily chapel services and discussed the sermons over cafeteria trays. He invited me to the cinema and helped me make the acquaintance of Federico Fellini, Ingmar Bergman and Stanley Kubrick. I was his guest for Thanksgiving dinner with some colleagues at the academy where he taught. He was an in-residence tutor filling the interstices of my undergraduate education. It turned out to be one of the most significant years of my life. Clark had no small part to play in my learning leap. It was a year in which, undergraduate degree notwithstanding, I was learning to be a student. I stepped from the strand and waded into the deeper waters of faith.

A major adjustment for me was living and studying in a racially diverse zip code. All of my previous experience had been in a racially homogenous culture. My abysmal ignorance and naiveté were confronted by attitudes I did not understand. The civil rights struggle was moving into high gear, and I was introduced to realities about which I had only read. One side of my cultural enlightenment was lovely, the other frightening; one side comfortable, the other disconcerting. I began to think about justice in different ways. It was one of the reasons I needed to come here.

I find myself in this season of life glancing as much in the rear view mirror as through the windshield. Looking back I now realize the bottom line of the debt I owe to people who were my colleagues, confessors, and co-conspirators. While time remains, for them and me, I must pay something on the due bill for my nurture. It is past time to acknowledge with thanks some extraordinary gifts.

I determined to tell Clark that our roommate year has come to mean far more to me than I ever realized at the time. I retrieved from memory the name of the school where he taught and wrote to the Dean, inquiring if she would be so kind as to provide me with a current address. Her gracious response was prompt. The Dean was sorry to inform me that Clark had died several years ago. She had checked with people who had been at the school for many years and learned that he was a highly respected chaplain and professor. There are several faculty members by whom he is fondly remembered. She wished she had better news to offer me. She thanked me for inquiring about Clark. Not for the first time, and not for the last, I arrived too late. I should have booked an earlier flight.

From my pocket, I remove my long and polished rosary of regrets. As my hands move over the familiar beads, I think that I might suggest an addition to the well-worn pairs recorded in the third chapter of Ecclesiastes: a time to receive and a time to give thanks. The door to gratitude is bound by time, open for an uncertain season: the fragile now. The only door before me opens on the hall of memory.

There is more sadness than guilt that I did not act upon the admirable intention I entertained over the years. I was grateful but did not let it be known. The gift was purchased and nicely wrapped but never delivered. The loss is mine; an opportunity squandered, now irreparable. I do not believe that Clark needed my gratitude, but I know what a gift it is when I discover that I have made a difference in someone's life. It is a gift I withheld, not intentionally, but by assuming tomorrow. The grace of God is sufficient for this and for me. I feel more admonished than convicted.

Nearly one-half century later the experience of meeting a Moravian from Utica is still teaching. I am still learning. I have some bills which are past due. There are some letters waiting be to written.

In memory of Clark Alva Thompson

REPENTANCE

As best I can remember I was twenty-three years old when I had my first sit-down conversation with a person of color. It was my second year of theological studies and Ralph's room was on the same floor as mine. It had taken me twenty-three years to get to this conversation, not because I had been consciously avoiding it, but because this was the first natural opportunity that had presented itself. I had never really tried before.

Almost all of my life before and after that conversation has been lived within a twenty-five mile circle in northeastern Pennsylvania. Not only had I never had a conversation with a person of color before, I had rarely even seen one. There were no people of color in my elementary, middle or high school, none in my church, none in my community and very few in my college.

Partly because I never encountered people of color and partly because I was raised in a home and school that taught that all people were equal, I believed that we were a people without prejudice or racism. We got to our feet as each school day began and affirmed that we believed in "liberty and justice for all." Week after week in Sunday school we happily sang our conviction that Jesus loves the little children, "red and yellow black and white, they are precious in His sight." We truly believed that in our heads and hearts.

When we spoke of prejudice at all it was to feel pity and disdain for those folks down South who did not treat "Negroes" fairly. We could afford to be smug because it cost us nothing. Arrogance is the name of a safe promontory from which to look down upon others. We believed that we had hearts, minds and doors that were open before it became a campaign.

And yet I clearly remember another, less savory, side to life on smug mountain. Even now I wince to recall the abundant racial humor. I was steeped in the popular mythology about the intelligence, athletic skill, musical ability, sexual prowess, and work ethic of people of color. I recall attitudes that surfaced when the civil rights movement began. It was not uncommon to overhear "What do those people want?

They are trying to get too much too quickly. They should be happy just to live in America. Their leaders are trouble makers. They are all Communists."

We were not bad people. In many cases we were very good people, at least no better or worse than those who had nothing to say. But racism is an equal opportunity infection that does not pass over good people for their goodness and settle only upon the evil for their sins. In ways I did not even understand I was infected. I still live with symptoms of that infection.

When I have personal experience with people of color, hear a language other than my own, see unfamiliar dress, read news accounts with photographs, sometimes one of my childhood myths calls from some slimy deep. I respond in ways that I do not believe, in ways contrary to what I teach and preach, in ways that show I am not the person I believe myself to be, in ways that reveal my need for repentance. In a moment of clarity I ask myself "where did that come from? Where in Hell did that come from?" And I learn something about myself. Sometimes I see that same darkness in the people around me. Racism is frequently subtle. It has a thousand disguises.

Few people of color in our geography worship in our churches or call our congregations "home." Businesses, corporations, and hospitals actively seek people of color to share their skills and abilities. Churches, with few exceptions, have not.

While a few pastors of non-white ethnic backgrounds have served our churches faithfully and with distinction, others have had very difficult experiences. Some pastors of color among us have met with hostility, derision and endless complaints. The gracious inclusiveness that we know as those who eat one loaf and drink one cup is withheld. The gifts and graces that they bring often go unnoticed or uninvited. We are frequently impatient with their use of English, their accents, their verbal cadences, their theology, their customs. We assume they have a lot to learn from us. We assume that they have little to teach us. We want to eliminate rather than celebrate our differences. Some people transfer their membership.

Laity of color who join our faith communities are generally welcomed but it is frequently with the expectation that they become like us as soon as possible. We are living comfortably in status quo and we resist change. We expect the newcomers to make the changes while we watch and wait in the back pews.

We are not bad people. In many ways we are extraordinarily good people. We can be repeatedly generous without complaint. We can be compassionate to a fault. We can hear the cry of the needy and travel to distance lands with our hearts on our sleeves and our hands open wide.

Most of us want to be free of racism, prejudice, and the injustice of white privilege. But some unfinished business clearly remains. I expect to be working on that unfinished business this side of casting crowns. There is a time for every purpose under heaven. It is time to hear God's gracious invitation to repent.

SCAVENGERS

Not so long ago I received the gift of some "free time." Both danger and opportunity, I choose the latter to make some additions to my life. My wife and I have added some daily walking in our neighborhood. Exercise allows at least the appearance of staying a furlong ahead of the pale horse. Heeding the admonition to "use it or lose it", we dress in layers appropriate to the day and set out in search of a little aerobic challenge, stretching some protesting joints and muscles. The jury it still deliberating on which charge, use or lose, we shall be convicted.

Our route is a largely uninhabited township road, euphemistically labeled "unimproved" on the local map. One residence on the route, an organic mélange of mobile home and miscellaneous outbuildings, made unique by the addition of graffiti, vehicles that formerly provided transportation, a rooster known only by his alarm, three tethered dogs, and various signs asserting that the land is "Posted" and any who might be tempted otherwise should know to "Keep Out." The size and temperament of the dogs make the signs redundant. The one dog that we hear but cannot see, a basso profundo, gets me to wondering if we might have stumbled upon Baskerville Hall. *Cave canem!*

Early in this regimen, we discovered what is unfortunately true of many rural American byways: roadside trash. A significant amount of the debris is aluminum cans representing the malted beverage preferences of our neighbors. What occurred to us almost at once was that we could bag the aluminum cans on our walks and deposit them in the collection barrel at our church. A member of our congregation gathers all the cans, transports them to the recycling center, realizes some profit from the effort, and donates the money to the amortization of the education-building mortgage.

Our effort has been going reasonably well. We have accumulated four and one-half large trash bags of crushed cans that we subsequently deposited in the church offering barrel. Roadside aluminum cans inexplicably replenish on a weekly basis. They reproduce in secret and escape though the windows of anonymous vehicles. We expect to have plenty of work in the days ahead unless the Volstead Act is renewed.

The whole enterprise is a feel-good, win/win experience in satisfying labor. How often in anyone's experience has any single activity had a triple benefit? There is physical fitness from the walk itself, environmental improvement from collecting roadside trash and a reduced mortgage from redeemed aluminum. It is unmitigated "yes" which would get any do-gooder's heart to singing, and it does. I look forward to our bag days because the outcome is so satisfying. We puzzle our neighbors, no doubt, as they observe our roadside mission and consider our need for one form of therapy or another. The stares notwithstanding, scavengers belong to an honorable guild.

I have been reflecting on why I enjoy this project so much. I believe that it has to do with the way I have invested my life for forty years. Those who have chosen to work with people and institutions inhabit a universe of delayed gratification. Those who work to enrich, reclaim, inspire, or rescue people have much more elusive yardsticks to measure success than those who fill the recycling barrel with scavenged aluminum. Teachers, preachers, social workers, counselors, parents, and countless other members of this extended tribe are planters of seed that they may never see germinate and grow.

Seeds grow in the dark, in secret, in silence, and in their own good season. This tribe plows, plants, fertilizes, waters, prunes, and prays for what they believe is happening out of plain sight. This tribe trades in hope, cultivates unrewarded patience, plays chess with fate, and by persistence masters a waiting game, as if they had any other choice.

Some of us also know this tribe as our faith family, sisters and brothers in a realm whose reality we hope is becoming more evident within us and among us. We are a family that gives ear to such encouragement as "let us not grow weary in doing what is right, for we will reap at harvest time, if we do not give up...whenever we have the opportunity let us work for the good of all."[5] We witness to a way that enriches, reclaims, inspires, and rescues, guiding people to a right relationship with God and each other. We witness to a shared vision that binds us together even though "this world with devils filled should threaten to undo us."[6] We witness to a long road made hopeful by fellow travelers. We witness to the difference between being successful and being faithful.

Now and again, it is good to have the immediate satisfaction of a harvest of aluminum cans, cleaner roadside and quickened pulse. It is one gentle reminder of a different harvest, known primarily in our dreaming, when the children of earth are safely gathered in, when the laborers can finally take their rest, and when everyone sits down together and shares the feast.

ARMS LENGTH

I t is an invitation that we have not been able to refuse. Against our
wishes, we have had the short course in hurricane meteorology.
We have listened to the Weather Channel teachers explain to us,
practically on an hourly basis, the formidable sequence from tropical
depression to powerful hurricane. We have watched as angry wind and
water appeared on stage in locales we normally associate with five star
resorts and luxury cruises. As spectators at any disaster, we have
craned our necks to get a better view of nature at the extremes. We
have been reminded of what it feels like to stand helpless before forces
over which we have no control, forces over which our power to
intervene is limited to celestial petition.

Many of us have not been disinterested spectators. We have family
and friends who are as helpless as we are, but with the added burden of
having homes in the line of wind, wave, high tide, and storm surge.
They are bewildered as friendly seas turn enemy. We have friends and
colleagues in Cuba and Haiti where resources for recovery are
practically nonexistent. By imagination, we have waited through the
night in basement or bathroom as winds dismantle the feckless shelters
we have constructed to protect us.

Heeding the evacuation warnings, the prudent escape to find a new
community of the dislocated in gymnasiums and fellowship halls.
Emergency workers shoulder the load for the rest of us. Horror grips
us as nature's fury further devastates some of the poorest of the poor in
our hemisphere. Those who merit nature's caress receive a backhand
instead. Our sighs and groans carry our prayers for mercy. Our checks
carry our unwillingness to allow nature the last word.

It is a season to store in memory, filed beside the other storms we
know by name and heart, floods to which we have added the water of
our own tears. Nature makes the rules in a game in which we are
required to have a seat on the sidelines. When the winds and waves
have had their say, we move back on stage and begin to act upon the
most fundamental of human urges: rebuild. Nature at its worst is an
unintended catalyst for community.

A few years ago, we were introduced to a hurricane Hugo. Wind and wave wrought havoc on coastal South Carolina. Traveling through the area several months after the devastation I heard Governor Carroll Campbell, Jr. recount the tale of his people's trial by wind and water in his state-of-the-state address.[7] He remembered touring the flooded area by helicopter. Many homes were under water. At one point the searchers noticed someone waving at them. A group of stranded men, women, and children in a schoolyard were desperately trying to get their attention by waving a red sweater.

The governor and his aides stopped and offered assistance to the several dozen people. They told an incredible nightmare of the previous night. As ocean waters began to invade, they were forced from their homes, taking refuge in a schoolhouse. When the surge tide flooded the school they were cut off from escape. As the waters continued to rise within the school they pulled desks to the center of the room and climbed upon them, getting above the water as best they could. The water continued to rise and, with no other choice, the adults took their children and lifted them above their heads. They held those children at arm's length to keep them above the waters. Mercifully, the water receded and tragedy was averted.

Governor Campbell said that the adults in the school that night were fully prepared to sacrifice everything in order to save their children. He told the story of those brave South Carolina parents to honor their character, courage and spirit.

The opening line of the Reformation Hymn sings within us as waters rise and winds dismantle. Luther affirms that God is a strong fortress, a reliable bulwark, a helper "amid the flood of mortal ills prevailing."[8] Mortal ills wear many costumes, natural and human. Mortal ills create their own realities. Mortal ills do not submit to reason or justice. Mortal ills are invisible to NOAA warnings and Doppler radar.

The tale of the South Carolina schoolhouse comes visiting in this season of hurricane, mortal ills delivered by wind and water. In our mind's eye, we can see parents on desktop, surrounded by storm surge, holding their children at arm's length above their heads, refusing to surrender what is most precious to a remorseless nature.

One person holding another at arm's length above the rising tide is an appropriate icon for the family we claim by adoption. It embodies our determination that others will not face the destructive powers, the mortal ills, alone. It is an icon which demonstrates an active compassion for the vulnerable, and it acknowledges that we are willing to pay some of the bill for each another, even as ours has been paid.

It is an icon with deep roots in our family, an icon that has the ability to transport us to another time and place, when someone with arms fully extended interposed himself for us, lifting humankind above the flood of mortal ills, making the way of the cross to be the path to life.

Because we know the blessed grace of surviving the storm surge, we pray for the grace and courage to extend our arms for others, so they will not have to face the rising tides alone.

FREE LUNCH

A friend sits across a lunch table and empties an overflowing heart. Nearing the end of her long and painful story, she finally says to me, "You know, when all of these things went wrong in my life, I thought it might help if I went to church. So I started. I came for quite a while. But my problems did not go away. My life did not get any better. Everything was just as bad as before. I figured, what's the use? So I stopped coming. It didn't seem to make any difference one way or the other. I might just as well sleep on Sunday morning."

My listening, my questions and my counsel do not seem to bring her any comfort. I wish I had healing words to change her mind, to help her stay with the congregation while she waits for the peace she seeks. As is so often the case, I am not able to fix what is broken. She musters in that regiment of the purple-hearted, the wounded who retreat in their pain and disappointment.

St. John remembers the day after the feeding of the 5,000 when the crowd pursued Jesus to his hiding place to force him to be king.[9] Here was a king who feeds by miracle and not by the sweat of the brow or the bend of the back. There were twelve baskets left over. He appeared to be a first century fish-in-every-pot king for all seasons. But in their enthusiasm a point was missed. They were yet to learn that he was not a smoke and mirrors wizard pulling ropes behind the curtain. He had something far more profound, more permanent, to offer them. Sometimes miracles can mislead.

When they finally track him down and invade his retreat he confronts them: "You come to me because of the loaves you ate, not because you saw signs."[10] They had come for another free lunch and not for the deeper feeding he was offering. And yet, who could blame them? We understand. We are at the head of the queue. Give us what we want, when we want it, or even promise it, and we too will invade his retreat. He spreads the feast before us–food for life, drink for life eternal, but we prefer to take our chances with the luncheon buffet.

Give us belly food over soul food every time. There is nothing wrong with belly food, of course, except that we are hungry an hour later.

When we are willing to let people cross our defenses they will tell us of that deep hunger: illness, infidelity, broken families, bankruptcy, addictions, untimely death, aging, emptiness and loneliness. They will tell us how they have prayed their hearts out to be rescued. They have asked God to stretch forth a mighty arm and make the cancer go away, the spouse stop drinking, the prodigal come home, and the numbers on the ping-pong balls roll their way for once—just this once.

It is not as hard to follow Jesus when all is well, when we eat our fill of bread and fish, when we are healthy, the kids are in the Honor Society, we are blessed by a happy marriage, we like our job, and we have a few bucks under the mattress. But what happens when the locusts ride in on a cold night wind and devour the crops?

A disappointed friend told me of her change in church attendance, not coming any more, believing that she understood that if she did her part, God would do God's part. She attends and God rescues. I understand. I hurt along with her. I have invaded Jesus' retreat with my empty baskets more than once. I hope and pray for her, and for myself, that the word about the deeper, hunger would capture our hearts and transform our desires. With the deeper hunger satisfied, we learn to live and grow with the other hungers.

My reading of the Gospel does not reveal any guarantee of rescue, although God's grace can and does afford it. It does not promise another free lunch, although life-transforming grace surely is free. I read about the promise of presence and possibility. I read of the bread of life that feeds the deepest human hunger for meaning and the wine that quenches the hidden thirst for life eternal. I read about the gift of a peace which remains after the locust's work is done.

The meal is not food or drink, rescue or windfall, success or good check-ups or anything else from which we might want God to deliver to us in our desire or our need. The meal is the grace of God. It can become more than a metaphor for us, a gift that keeps on giving. And if that grace were all that we ever received, it would be enough.

FOOLISHNESS

The BBC mystery series was very well written, acted, and directed. It fact, it was among the very best DVD drama I had seen in some time. As I was reflecting on what I had been enjoying I was hectored by a palpable discomfort. In many of the episodes a clergyman is a character in the script, sometimes a larger role, sometimes lesser. But what became increasingly clear to me was that the writers were having their say about the Christian Church and its clergy. It was primarily the Anglicans to be sure, but I could not escape the conviction that Christians in general were being painted with the same brush.

In virtually every episode where clergy were present he was male, older, a bit overweight, in clerical haberdashery, and serving a small, passive congregation. Furthermore, the clergyman was never presented in any role that we would remotely admire or choose to emulate. In one case the clergyman was a spy. In the other cases, he may have been well-meaning but hopelessly out-of-touch with the real world around him. The series clergy were living in their own little world. That world was hopelessly beside the point for what mattered in the stories. It some cases they were silly. In other cases they were clueless. They were either fools or rascals. In all cases they were superfluous.

The realization made me wince. We have all seen or heard similar accounts. The church, indeed religion in general, is an easy target. Once again the church was taking some licks. Organized religion, if not the faith it represents, was being made to look foolish.

The writers were playing it for laughs, or something more sinister. They put a rogue's gallery of religious stereotypes on parade. While I would not deny that some elements were plausible, it appeared to me to be shooting fish in a barrel. Popular culture has done us few favors. When it attempts to portray religious faith in a sympathetic vein it typically ends up with sentimental drivel or a magical mystery tour of new age fantasies. When it is less than sympathetic, we are portrayed as rogues, duplicitous con artists or dumber-than-dirt folks without a prayer of convincing a cynical world. We are fodder for entertainment and vilification alike. All of that notwithstanding, I don't look to the popular culture to preach the Gospel that has been entrusted to us.

I would love to believe that this terrible disconnect between the Gospel to which we lay claim and the way in which an unbelieving world sees us is the fault of the sinister, demon-infested board rooms and back rooms of the media decision-makers. Some of that may be true. But I cannot rationalize it all that easily. My discomfort with the series got me pondering the church's culpability in the poor public persona from which we suffer.

If St. Paul is to be believed, appearing foolish in the eyes of the world is an honorable estate. To lay claim to a vocation as a "fool for Christ" is a high calling indeed.[11] If I were ever accused of being such a fool I doubt that enough evidence could be produced to convict me. There are not that many of us worthy to be judged such a fool. Generally we meet them as saints and martyrs, giving their lives away in holy abandon. But our foolishness in the eyes of the world, I am afraid, is too often for the wrong reasons. We have squandered our foolishness on that which is unworthy of that calling, the worst kind of prodigality.

Writer Frederick Buechner writes that there are two kinds of fools. We can either be damned fools or we can be fools for Christ's sake.[12] Too often the world sees in us the former and not the latter. Too often we are known by a false gospel of success, denominational competition, hoarded financial resources, timidity in the face of injustice, Gospel words substituting for Gospel deeds, exclusion, bigotry, closed minds, closed doors, closed hearts, and naiveté about what people really need. In terms of the Gospel of Jesus Christ that is indeed foolishness, but it is not that to which St. Paul's challenges us. It is not the holy foolishness likely to bring an unbelieving world within earshot of the Gospel.

For the sake of Christ we could be known as the people who give it all away, as those for whom no one is taken to be lost forever, as those whose hospitality is spontaneous and unrelenting, as those whose arms encompass all the children of earth, as those who measure ministry not by what they have but by what they share, as those to whom no human is a stranger, as those to whom the only enemy is injustice and its sinful cohorts, as those indifferent to class, status, race, and gender and as those willing to lose everything in order to gain Christ. Sometimes that is who we are; often it is not. In the eyes of the world we will appear foolish no matter what we do.

Cheap shot notwithstanding, the series writers had the effect of stirring within me a desire to ponder holy foolishness. I called to mind the company of those who are a living mystery, who touch and handle things unseen, whose lives can only be explained because of their passion for God. In my imagination I entertained for a time those wonderfully wise fools who have carried our faith family on their shoulders through the ages. And in that moment I wanted to make my foolishness matter. Even at a safe distance, I hope I never lose sight of them.

You just never know when those who are trying to make you look foolish might be offering you a blessing in disguise.

VALENTINE

It was a unanimous vote. The congregation had been offered the option of a secret ballot but there was no need. No "nays." No abstentions. A silent show of hands was sufficient. To arrive at this destination the congregation had waded into a rising tide of reality for more than a year. The real decision preceded the vote by weeks, probably months, perhaps years. There was a simple resolution, a few questions and little discussion. The folks were ready to vote and move on.

During the prelude one saint leaned over and whispered, "What a beautiful sanctuary. This is the first time I have ever been here in the daylight." True enough, visitors were blessed by wood, stained glass and smiling faces that made them welcome. Saints on earth and saints above gathered in this unfamiliar place thanks to the hospitality of this sister congregation. It was a place of welcome and grace conducive to "yes." An inaudible sigh of release could be heard by those with ears for the hearing. The congregation assembled in respect of known and unknown saints upon whose shoulders, perhaps even backs, they knew they were standing.

They were guests here because their own sanctuary was unfit for any worship service, the ceiling having collapsed in the quiet of the night. Mercifully, their sanctuary was entertaining no living souls at the time. Plaster and beams gave way from sheer fatigue. Generations of song, candle fumes, prayers of confession, John 3:16, the laughter of children, the sweet perfume of grape juice and the exquisite aroma of Welsh Cookies on the griddle were condensed in the heights. If any of the members had been waiting for a final sign to guide the future, the wooden pews buried in ceiling pointed the way. It was the morning after the second night when Gideon spread the fleece.

The church building is a distinguished senior resident in a changing urban neighborhood. The twin towers are a prominent skyline feature on that side of the city. Those towers give witness to a time when the sanctuary was full and the church school overflowed. Black and white photographs and a full trophy case in the fellowship hall testify to former days of proud congregational memory. Ministry and mission once moved from sanctuary and classroom to community and world. Current reality had come to mock that memory. Extraordinary needs of the church building were beyond even imagined remedies. For the remaining faithful few the needs of the building forged an unholy alliance with declining resources. No choice, only choice and right choice were married.

Faced with the same challenge as many other churches, urban and rural, the congregation owned the truth from the not-too-distant future that was racing to meet them. Responsible stewardship demanded that they liberate the church from the building. They had become the servants of the building that had once served them. Theirs had become a ministry of building maintenance. The vote was unanimous. The building was to be given to another congregation that wanted and needed it. The beloved home of one congregation was now to be loved by another.

The legacy of mission and ministry in that place would be carried on by other disciples of the same Lord. The name on the outside bulletin board and the racial make-up of the congregation would change; the same Lord would be served. No change would be needed in the Foundation. It was a painful and faithful decision. They chose to surrender the sacred space of a thousand sacred stories. Holy water tears flow from the springs of memory to irrigate the seeds of another future, their own and that of others. Tears of sadness and hope mingled as we stood to sing "God of Grace and God of Glory, on thy people pour thy power."

There is no "one size fits all" when it comes to discerning God's purposes for a particular congregation. Living faithfully into God's future might mean setting the building aside or it might mean claiming a new vision for those same old structures. Prayerful discernment is the vehicle for that journey.

The writer of Hebrews admonishes, "Lay aside every weigh which clings so closely and run with perseverance the race set before us."[13] Weights come in a variety of sizes and shapes but they can all be anchors in the race. Weights might even be as massive as a beloved building. After the most careful study, broad consultation and prayerful discernment the congregation came to understand that it can be as faithful to let go as to hang on. God had something else in store for them.

As the organist played "Jesus Loves Me" the one child at worship returned to her seat clutching a valentine.

HOSPITALITY

Approaching the main entrance to the church, I assumed that the blankets and clothing piled haphazardly along the sidewalk were assorted debris that the janitor had not yet collected and properly placed in the Dumpster. I had a flash of wonder if they might be the worldly possessions of some anonymous homeless person, but I dismissed that as unlikely. Homeless people don't sleep under trees on the front lawn of churches, at least the churches with which I was familiar.

We were on an all-day mission trip to see some of the saints on the front lines of ministry in the city. This was the fourth of our five stops. The building, an attractive but tired old fortress, suggested glories past when middle-class white folks paid the bills. The pastor was a diminutive woman who came to the United States from the Philippines. She and her laity told us what it meant to be a sanctuary for souls in that quarter of urban poverty, illiteracy, crime and hopelessness. The pastor's height and Spanish accent could deceive you into thinking that she might have bitten off more than she could chew of urban decay. But if the mind went there it would be wrong.

Pastor Santiago remembered her first year in the church when the building was broken into and robbed ten times. She rehearsed the constant battle to cover over the ubiquitous graffiti spray-painted on the building. It had to be done. You could not yield to the forces that deface, intimidate, threaten, undermine, mock and destroy.

Finally, when she told us of the two teenage boys who were shot to death on the front sidewalk of the church, her voice broke. For a moment she lost her composure as the pain of the tragedy came calling once again. As she wiped tears she said to us, "There is so much evil in the world. God has placed us here to resist that evil and overcome it with good." She pleaded with us: "We need you. Won't you help us struggle against that evil?"

She confessed, and her whole body smiled, that it was a privilege to pastor that loving congregation. She said that her people truly welcomed everyone who came to them. They practiced the hospitality

115

of the Gospel. She spoke to us of her small multi-cultural, multi-lingual, multi-ethnic, immigrant congregation. The welcome mat was out for any and all human beings in search of the means of grace.

The clothing piled by the door belonged to Carol, "our homeless woman" who, in spite of being taken to a shelter many times, always found her way back to the church. They fed her when she was hungry and let her sleep in the churchyard. The clothing and bedding by the walkway were sacred objects, symbols of authentic discipleship. The church militant was on view here before God and anyone who cared enough to look.

Confronted by an honest-to-God saint my thin veneer of comfortable Christianity seemed a mockery of those who follow Jesus in deed as well as word. She didn't intend it but there was no way not to stand convicted by my own mediocre discipleship. What was most persuasive to me about this ministry, however, was her passion. Her plain words in accented English, her beloved laity standing with her in the fellowship hall, the bedding by the front walk, unqualified hospitality for all God's children, the absolute determination of those saints to be faithful to Christ, and their refusal to be cowed by evil, called powerfully to my spirit. And in that moment the meaning of being a disciple of Jesus Christ was as transparent to me as it had ever been.

Those saints labor on in their vineyard. I thank God for them. I return to the vineyard that I have been given to tend. And while my garden is different in so many ways from theirs, I don't know if my tending could ever be quite the same again.

The pastor rhetorically asked if we would join her and her flock in resisting the evil that mocks God's love. There could be no answer other than "yes."

ORDINARY TIME
ON THE ROAD

SENSELESS

Even at this distance, several years and thousands of miles accumulated, I still occasionally pause to wonder why I was the recipient of a random act of senseless kindness. Midsummer, I was piloting a vanload of adolescents to the start of a week's worth of church camp. The Massachusetts Turnpike was just another hot, crowded interstate with miles to go before we could unload the van, pitch our tents and inflate our air mattresses. The pilot was tired, resisting road ennui and stressed with the stewardship of precious cargo, seat-belted and quietly dozing in the rear.

Merging into the queue at one of the all-too-frequent tollbooths, I finally faced the attendant and through an open window extended the ransom to lift the gate and let us proceed. The smiling woman waved me through with the words, "the car ahead of you paid your toll." I must have looked sufficiently incredulous that she needed to repeat the words of absolution. Go in peace, your debt is forgiven. Was there some mistake? Bemused, I moved forward into the flow of traffic and gradually got back up to speed.

The anonymous doer-of-the-deed was long gone. I could not tell you anything about the vehicle or its driver. The random kindness did, however, set in motion an obsession to know why someone had selected us to benefit from this unmerited gift. Why were we singled out to have our debt cancelled on a summer road far from home? I spent my musing time on the rest of that trip pondering the answer to that mystery. It became a topic of campfire conversation.

It was not the amount of the toll that captured me, but why it had been paid at all. What was the motivation for such behavior toward strangers? I continue to speculate about it but I expect to never know. The answer is not important. The act of random kindness has worked its deeper purpose. Such is the power of a random kindness to plant its transforming seed in the recipient. It is a minor tear in the fabric of business as usual. A thumb presses on one side of the balance scale. Some of the laborers in the vineyard have more in their pay envelopes than they earned.

I have been reflecting on the bond forged by that one act of random kindness. I have no idea if the toll-payer ever again wondered about the vanload of campers on the Mass Pike. Perhaps that person regularly sprinkles such seeds and we were just one planting in a lifelong garden. It calls to mind that remarkable tale by Jean Giono about a dauntless shepherd who planted acorns which in time transformed a wasteland into a paradise.[1] I suspect that we were just a transplant on the highway that afternoon. I now name another teacher whose name I do not know.

The power of that summer tollbooth, a fracture of the expected, was no less than the power of every unmerited gift, the power of every grace, to change the receiver. Whenever obvious justice is made to stand on its head heaven opens a crack and offers a glimpse of the true heart at the center of the universe. Whenever our debt is cancelled, our ransom paid, the "get-out-of-jail free" card dealt from the deck, or the tollbooth attendant waves us through, we know again that of which our baptism is prime token.

Sometimes we experience the mystery of the toll already paid. When it happens it is practically guaranteed to transport us to another place. We traffic with the unseen. We smile as we toss our hat into the air. We would swear we can taste bread and wine. We remember that we are never far from the table, never far from the Host. It is not so random after all.

HOMELESS

I did a quick lateral to avoid stepping on him. An ignored body impeded the busy urban sidewalk. His need positioned him so he would not be overlooked. Several strides beyond him he registered on the radar of my conscience. He was begging outside one of those exquisite import shops. Jewelry without price tags called through the alarmed window to urban professionals on mission elsewhere. He was curled fetal, asleep during rush hour, something unwanted left behind. Beside him, a blue plastic disposable cup with a few coins was in plain view. A child-scrawl-hand-lettered piece of cardboard announced two of the current stigmas that separate the children of earth: *Homeless – AIDS.* If the left one doesn't get you, then the right one will. The disposable plastic cup was icon of far more than a coin holder.

My spontaneous response was avoidance. Not only did I not want to hurt him, but I also wanted some safe zone between his need and its claim upon me. I knew that I did not want him to cross into my world or me into his. After all, I was only a visitor in this place. This is not my town. This is not my job. This is not my problem. At that moment my only problem was how to rationalize my way out of any responsibility.

Affliction can be so overwhelming that a person becomes a thing, not a "thou" but an "it." We are bewildered when the need cannot be rationalized, denied or ignored. How do we respond to affliction that is in our face or under our feet? On that pavement, that day, I was one of thousands who passed him. My pity, pocket change and prayer left him unchanged as far as I could tell. If only some combination of those could have opened the door to health and home.

He never saw me. I still see him. I did not recognize him but I knew who he was. Perhaps it was his resemblance to the blank faces that look back at me through the fences in the refugee camps, the swollen bellies of starvation, the HIV children, the un-faired against, the bruised and battered, and the familiar strangers who knock on the door of my life. In his face I see all those for whom the tears of God continually water the earth. For them the tears of heaven and earth flow together.

I prayerfully muse if I shall see him again along with his countless, nameless brothers and sisters. I do not lose sight of that reunion promised in Matthew 25, an exam for which we spend a lifetime preparing.[2] I know well enough that it is not the whole Gospel, but that won't let me avoid its truth. If the incarnation is true, it seems to me that the presence of the Christ in every human is true as well. Anyone who is confidently prepared for that final exam needs to be admonished. The hero with a thousand faces is the Lord of a million disguises. According to Matthew, that disguise is affliction.

It takes very little self-examination to confront the truth that when the sheep and the goats claim their ultimate inheritance, mine is with the goats. How could it be otherwise if I am accountable for the affliction I have denied, rationalized, judged, ignored, or handed off to providence and professionals? If my acts of compassion and mercy are the only presentation I can make at the gathering of the nations, then the outcome is guaranteed. Thank God I am not my own final judge.

And yet my heart is not with the goats. I have a sheep's heart, a sheep's desire, and a sheep's dreams. I am a sheep wannabe. I am not content to deny and rationalize and side step, tempting as that usually is. I will continue to do it, of course, but I am not satisfied with my behavior. I repent of it. I too claim St. Paul's conundrum of being simultaneously bound by flesh and spirit.

I was not able to save "Homeless" with my pity, my pocket change and my prayer. But perhaps our meeting was one of the signs that a gracious God has not stopped watering my fruits-of-the-spirit tree. One thing for sure, "homeless" and I will be meeting again.

HELL

I am a stranger here; no one you would know. Anonymity has it
charms as expectations diminish all around. I am a long way from
home on this Sunday morning. Distance notwithstanding, it feels
like I have been here before. Greeted by the "greeters", settled into my
air-conditioned-cushioned-pew, midway down the left hand side of the
sanctuary, I watch the regular congregation gradually claim customary
spaces. The familiars greet one other and catch up on this and that. My
solitude is honored and the congregation does not permit any curiosity
about the stranger to overcome its reticence.

The organist begins the prelude, a seamless conjunction of hymn
tunes, the words for which a hymnal was unnecessary. The amplitude
of conversation correlates positively with the organ volume. I examine
the bulletin in anticipation of what lies ahead. No surprises in sight,
my comfort level rises and I give myself permission to put full weight
down on my anonymous solitude. I give thanks for the precious
moments to center in silent prayer.

We are presently informed that the preacher of the morning is a
substitute invited into the need, the appointed pastor recovering from
illness at home. I suspect that his precise English accent would sound
erudite even if he were reading a grocery list. The sermon text is
selected portions of John 14, Jesus' farewell to his companions:
familiar, beloved and without obvious surprises.

Having been sent into this game from the bench myself on more
than one occasion, I completely empathize and forgive that the
preaching does not appear to suffer from an abundance of preparation.
The exposition of scripture is correct but not arresting. My attention
takes wing as I count exposed organ pipes and analyze stained glass
window symbols.

We sit for the offering, stand for the doxology and it appears we
shall momentarily be dismissed into the remains of the morning. The
preacher announces the final hymn: "When We All Get To Heaven."
In an unrehearsed moment, motivated by what I take to be his palpable
discomfort at allowing us to leave the sanctuary in happy, heavenly

anticipation, he spontaneously offers what I immediately know is the reason I was here this morning: "But we don't need to wait till we get to heaven. We can bring some heaven right now to those who are living in hell on this earth." And I thought I was safely out of here. The preacher's extemporaneous homily closes the exit and I am apprehended in the act of trying to keep my distance: *in flagrante delicto.*

You just never know when you show up for one of these family reunions who will take hold of your sleeve as you shirk toward the exit. I board the Subaru, but not without a hitchhiker inviting himself along for the ride. I take the long way home, pondering "those who are living in hell on this earth."

I spend a relatively small amount of time reflecting on hell as either geography or spiritual condition. Evenhanded in my treatment, I spend no greater time wondering about the promised joys of heaven. I am content to live the mystery. There is something in knowing that is not quite as wonderful as not knowing. Whenever hell or heaven intrude into my awareness I am usually on my way to some other destination. This morning, the substitute with the precise accent grabbed my lapels, looked me in the face and suggested that today would be a good day to add a stop on my itinerary. I wish that I could say I was grateful.

Hell usually breaks into my awareness as my anger spikes in the face of some news reporting an evil monstrosity gratuitously inflicted upon the innocent, the defenseless, the young or the dispossessed. I find myself earnestly wishing that I could register the guilty for Hell to punish such depravity for eternity: justice without mercy in the great rotisserie down below. As I wade through my anger I sometimes find the grace to ask God to turn my desire for punishment to a desire for redemption. Sometimes I remind myself that anger may satisfy, but it does not nourish. Sometimes I just stay very angry.

This morning, however, I am not moved by anger, punishment, or justice but by an intrusion of the suffering from which I manage generally to keep a safe distance. Hell is not an inappropriate metaphor for the lives of many of God's children near and far. My mind draws in people and places that suffer broken lives, broken economics, broken politics, broken priorities, broken religion, broken promises and broken compassion. Some of that is usually broken in me at least.

Hell is not a condition or a place that is within my power to cancel. That does not mean that I am without any power. I can still share the resources with which God has entrusted me among those who languish in their need: prayer, money, time, and a story. At least some will have a cup of cold water. At least some will hear of wondrous love. At least some will know the taste of bread and wine.

The substitute with the English accent was reminding those who were listening one Sunday morning to make sure that we include hell as one of the stops on our faith journey.

A VOICE FROM BEYOND

"**S**pecial This Week: Double Room $19.95." Someone had left the light on for us, or so it seemed. We had been driving all day, a hot and humid 650 miles. We had no reservation, figuring we would just find a place when we grew tired of the Interstate. We had our eye out for something familiar, some logo that might intimate clean and safe. By 10 PM, with no dinner other than a few Fig Newtons and some warm water, melted ice cubes from the last WaWa, we were willing to entertain an invitation from a stranger.

The question was, "how much motel will $19.95 buy?" Would we have the room to ourselves or would we be asked to share it with some other travelers or perhaps some local fauna? We sat with the engine idling while we did a remote interrogation of the façade before us. Could the price be too low? Our natural skepticism prevailed: too good to be true and it probably was. We U-turned back to the access road. Surely, there would be other choices further on so we could at least have a choice. There was very likely an even better deal on down the way.

Five rural miles later, the road less traveled, we understood that there were no other choices. A few shuttered farmhouses and a closed gas station dismissed our hope. $19.95 was the only game in town. Another U-turn, another five-mile return and we found ourselves in the original parking lot staring at the sign that read, "Special This Week: Double Room $19.95." However, it now had a brightly illuminated subscript: "No Vacancy." It is a tale told by travelers who could not foresee an offer withdrawn, an invitation rescinded, or the only choice to be right at hand. The best deal in town is often a moveable feast. Sometimes the hype of the sideshow barker is true, "for this one time only."

Alone among the Evangelists, Luke records Jesus' parable of the Rich Man and Lazarus.[3] In death, the rich man desires to amend his neglect of Lazarus while they both walked the earth. The rich man had opportunities to change Lazarus' situation in life and consequently his own situation in death. However, the distance between the two men in this life continued into the next. The rich man now wanted to close that distance but the opportunity had forever taken leave. The character of Abraham in the parable speaks of the "great chasm" that has been "fixed" between one life and the next. The opportunities in one do not extend into the other: for this one time only.

If only we could know how long a window will remain open, how long an offer will continue on the table, how long the stock will appreciate, how long the vacancy sign will be out, how long a person who loves us will wait for us to get our act together, how long we will have to splint a fractured relationship, or how long we will draw breath. Opportunities exist for the time being. No one can be sure when the loan will finally come due.

Among my saddest experiences over the years has been dealing with families and friends that have allowed chasms to open between them, canyons of enmity that separate parent from child, brother from sister, and friend from friend. The original causes of the fracture are often forgotten, the initial disappointment or anger replaced by a stubborn, self-righteous refusal to seek a way back. The saddest of all is when death intervenes to end all possibility of forgiveness and reconciliation. Grief, guilt, and regret become the ponderous legacy of those who remain. Tearstains on my office carpet accompany the sobs and words, "if only I had known." We weep together for what has been lost. The window of reclamation is closed.

A long-standing favorite movie of mine is *Field of Dreams*. A baseball tale serves as a canvas to paint a lovely dream about a time and place where people get another chance to fix what is broken, to choose a road not taken, and to learn from those who walk on another shore. It is a fantasy that strikes a deep cord within us because we wish that it could be so. We long to have another opportunity to get it right. We believe that we would be wiser this time. The film is a modern parable about the one-way, one-time road we all travel. But as the lights come up we realize that we only get to do it over again in the movies.

There are many lessons to a parable, of course. There are many layers to excavate and ponder. The tale of one man wishing he could do it over again, have another chance, get it right this time, does more to challenge than condemn. The windows of opportunity are open all the while. They come to us as an endless array set before us while we draw breath. They bring with them their own set of urgencies, from an offer too good to be true to a broken heart awaiting a healing word.

The parable cautions that we should not expect someone to return from the dead to admonish us on the urgent difference between finite and infinite. The parable asserts that we would not believe such a one even if it were allowed. And yet, the parable itself is a voice from beyond the grave. It is one more plea, one more prayer, another call to the one-time-only opportunities set before us. It is an invitation to entertain the possibility of the ultimate making its home within the ordinary.

PASSENGER

I am not an atheist. I can't remember a time in my life when that was a serious consideration. From time to time I have read the travel brochures, but I have never been tempted to purchase a ticket. Time out of mind, I booked passage on another ship on which I have been traveling my whole life. Before I knew what it was to know, inclinations were planted within me that, when the time was right, led me to the ticket agent and, for an exchange of considerations, I boarded and found my seat with the others.

If opinion research is to be believed, it is a ship with many passengers. In fact, the overwhelming majority of Americans say that they are on board. Polls reveal that about 90 percent of our fellow citizens say they believe in God. To be sure, the polls also reveal that only about 36 percent of that same group attends worship at least once each month. The current cliché is "I am spiritual but not religious." Belief is one thing, behavior is another; spirit and flesh always uneasy companions.

The ship stops from time to time to board and discharge. Sometimes I prefer the cabin and sometimes the deck. Across open seas and in port, through calm and storm, as human and natural disasters scroll in and out of view, I see things through the windows, and I hear things around me that have me checking my ticket. I beg what I need from other passengers. I give what I can when others ask. The ship is full in both joy and heartache. Nevertheless, my faith-doubt struggles invariably return me to the same starting point. I find myself standing with Simon Peter: "Lord, to whom can we go? You have the words of eternal life."[4]

Boarding this vessel is not the end of faith as much as the beginning. I consider what evidence I might offer to prove that I have been a passenger. I ponder worship attendance, bank statements, resume, the witness of friends, the testimony of family, the times I said "yes", the times I said "no", and the times I said nothing. Works do not save, of course, but I should be able to lay some harvest of the spirit upon the table. In any case, a search for fruit is an invitation to humility of spirit. There is no way to take that test but to bend the knee of the heart.

The memory of a beloved colleague pulls up a chair and makes itself at home. I find myself entertaining the longer thoughts. What sticks in my head, God knows why, is an ancient invitation or, more particularly, a plea: "I am offering you life and death, blessing and curse. Choose life, then, so that you and your descendants may live."[5] It was once issued to wilderness travelers in search of their promised home. Perhaps it is heard most clearly by those in search of home. Our choice pretty much determines whether we get there or continue to wander. Life and blessing were the choices of my colleague. He was a member of the crew on this ship. I breathe in the inspiration of his well-done.

I consider what it means to choose life and not death, blessing and not curse. I am quite certain that it is a choice not made once and done. There is always a response to be made to what I see from the deck and what I learn from the other passengers. But desiring to make the choice for life does not necessarily make it so. Often as not, I get it wrong.

The desire to choose life and not death begins in a mysterious center, a deep interior room, where all that is true about us makes itself known. It is the place where the sighs too deep for words are born. Sometimes it is seen in that partial disguise that we call our character. The choice for life and not death is made in the thoughts, in the imagination, in the dreams, in what we do and fail to do, in what we bless and what we curse. It is the "I" that is always in need of redemption, always in need of perfecting, always in need of forgiveness, and always in need of companions.

In grateful wonder I glance around at my fellow passengers. I call to mind the others, here and gone, seen and unseen, remembered and forgotten, friends on earth and friends above, and I smile. From that mysterious center I am overtaken by an unspeakable gratitude for the ones who helped me hear the invitation to board this ship. They live in sacred memory. That gratitude is also for those still with me on board, those who sustain and encourage me with their grace, their wisdom and their integrity. I cannot make this voyage alone.

My hand reaches into my pocket to close around a well-worn ticket. Until we make port there is more life and blessing to choose.

In memory of Franklin E. Kooker

SHADE

T he Ultraviolet Index (UV) for most days during my visit is typically 10. An additional explanation in the morning paper notes that an exposure level of 10 means that the risk is "very high". Occasionally the index reaches an 11, a signal of "extreme risk. The National Weather Service and the Environmental Protection Agency developed the UV Index as a way to help people plan their outdoor activities in order to avoid overexposure to UV radiation and the adverse health effects that accompany it.

I am unaccustomed to seeing regular reports of the UV Index in my part of the world. As far as I know, there is no Overcast Index (OC) but, given the minimal sunshine that we generally experience locally, I suppose one could be created to tell folks what we already know. With a little imagination, I am sure that we could develop a list of the adverse health effects that accompany the OC Index. A day with a forecast of OC 10 might mean, for example, that we need to take some extra vitamin D, make a telephone call to a good friend, or replay the Easter portion of Handel's *Messiah*.

My summer stay in the South means that I am experiencing serious sunshine as well as its traveling companions of heat, humidity, dehydration, and discomfort. I also discover the rationale and appreciation for the UV Index. The word "scorching" has an unfamiliar taste on my tongue but still becomes part of my casual conversation. I find myself moving as expeditiously as possible from one air-conditioned setting to another. I purchase one of those dashboard solar shades to inhibit the sun from cooking the interior of the Subaru. A new pre-exit checklist from home inserts itself into all travel plans: hat, sunglasses, SPF 30 sunscreen, and water bottle.

When it is necessary to be outside for any extended period I learn to scan the immediate vicinity and then move instinctively into whatever shade is available. Standing in direct sunlight for more than a few minutes is antagonistic to my pale northern skin. I watch construction workers with respect and admiration for their strenuous physical labor in full sun. I think of sun and shade in ways that are new to me. A short mantra takes up residence in my head, repeating itself during my outdoor excursions: shun sun, seek shade.

In the heat of the day, some other words surface and step to the front of the stage to have their say:

The Lord is your keeper/the Lord is your shade at your right hand. The sun shall not strike you by day/nor the moon by night.[6]

The Psalmist sings a song that is born in a land with UV exposures of 10 and above all the time. In his land having your parade rained upon is an occasion for doxology. It is the poetry of those who believe that too much sun or too much moon is hazardous: sunstroke and lunacy. For the Psalmist, to say that shade is salvation is no mere alliteration or metaphor. In the desert, shade is a matter of life and death.

The poetry expresses a deeper truth than just shade trees or overhanging rocks at high noon. When the Psalmist claims a word to embrace the essential saving presence of God in life, the chosen word is shade. That idea is particularly potent in a hostile, sun-drenched landscape. One particular word has the power to signify God's all-encompassing protection and succor. There are shades of shade: one offers shelter from fierce sunshine, another offers sanctuary on the lee of life-storms. Shade grants time to rest, to heal, and to prepare to return to full light.

Scurrying from one overhang to another, avoiding UV 10 at noonday, I reflect upon times and seasons when I prayed for shade. I remember days and nights when one fever or another overwhelmed my feeble defenses, when some sun or moon was threatening, in full light or in restless dreams. I recall with gratitude that the shade that found me usually came as a surprise, a gift and a saving grace. Invariably, the shade had a name: family, friend, sister, brother, colleague, stranger, saint, or angel. God's shade has many disguises, countless names and faces stand with us unawares. They come to us unbidden and incognito, spreading their gracious shelter above us, inviting us in, and patiently keeping watch until we discern the way forward.

133

We do not create the shade we need. We simply place ourselves under it, indeed within it, when it finds us. Shade is a blessing, the presence of the Holy One, in whom we moor in sun and moon. Night and day, day and night, there is always that same healing shadow, an oasis for all of God's children.

THIEVES

I was in search of something I had intentionally placed in a secure and easily remembered location. I have been here before. In this case, it was my camera. I had recorded in its digital locker a series of photos accumulated over more than one month. They were a progress report on some work I was doing. I was now ready to see and to share what I had been saving. By an orderly process of accessing the memory files in my brain I was confident that I had placed the camera in the glove compartment of the car. When I visited that place, however, the Canon did not answer the roll call. I was quite certain that is where I had stored it, but it was not to be found.

Since I am aware that my memory is often unreliable in these matters, I was now required to conduct an additional search of all of the other likely places where the camera might be hiding. Usually, when the missing item finally steps forward, I find it exactly where I had left it. But this extended search was not fruitful. The camera had, by one means or another, taken leave.

At last I remembered that, for the best of reasons, I had entrusted the car into the hands of strangers. One of those anonymous strangers had evidently opened the unlocked glove box and removed the easily concealable camera. My search had taken far more time than would allow any hope of recovery. I reluctantly but inexorably came to the conclusion that the Canon had been stolen by a person who had been the temporary steward of my car. This unknown person lived in a state 1,300 miles away. In a few moments it had become clear to me that I no chance of ever recovering the stolen camera.

Stealing is wrong. It needs to be prevented, prosecuted and punished. Stealing weakens civilized society. Thieves are a menace to what is decent and orderly. Once again I learn that it is only a few millimeters from the discovery of the theft to my anger. When people take from us we feel violated. There is a sense that it is not fair: "I trusted you; I did nothing to deserve this." I dine on my anger for a while. It feels good but is not very nourishing.

The camera can be replaced. In fact, it already has. It is a nuisance to be sure and some financial loss. But no one was injured and the worst for me was another case of twin disappointments: my own lack of prudence and some brother or sister taking advantage of me. It is just one more story to remind me of the reality of the world through which we are passing. It is one additional reminder that I might need to reconsider my reluctance to lock up, lock out and lock down. By any account I am far too trusting. I am foolish enough to hope that people will behave honorably when they are trusted. Those who keep trying to walk the balance beam between serpents and doves need to get accustomed to wearing black and blue.

For reasons I cannot say, the missing camera called to mind other times in my adult life when I have been a victim of theft. I ruefully recall one thing or another over the years that have been taken from me by stealth. Strangely enough, looking back now, I realize that I have made my way through life perfectly well without the stolen objects.

No one has ever been physically damaged, all of my financial losses were relatively small, and I did the requisite reporting to authorities when that made sense. So far I have managed to outrun the paranoia that often knocks on my door in the face of being more vulnerable than I had believed. I ponder lessons learned over the years when thieves broke in to steal my treasures on which moth and rust were dining. Unknown persons have sometimes inadvertently lightened my load. It may be that the thieves have rendered me a service.

Stealing is one of those universally proscribed acts that virtually every culture denounces and punishes. The Eighth Commandment as well as evangelists Matthew, Mark and Luke remembers that Jesus says that the commandment to not steal, among others, must be observed by those who want to "inherit" eternal life.[7] In Romans, St. Paul sharply admonishes his readers about preaching against stealing but stealing all the same.[8]

I occasionally try to imagine the persons who have taken from me over the years. In some cases there was a strong suspicion of the ones who broke, cut, entered and took. I never felt constrained to either play detective or to make unsubstantiated accusations. In other cases the thieves were and always will remain anonymous. I ponder their reasons for stealing and in so doing I open a wider door to enter.

Although I have never broken and entered a home, or smashed and grabbed, or mugged another person with threat of violence, there have been times when, by one means or another, I have taken what was not given to me. There have been other times when by silence or inaction I have been complicit in stealing by others.

The impulse to steal is alive and well especially if we believe that we will never be found out. So human an animal, we follow the lead of the orchard thieves who took it upon themselves to take and eat fruit that was not theirs. The apple does not fall far from the tree. Any accusations we make we make in a mirror.

I am long past any need or desire to find or punish those who have taken from me. In the end they took nothing of any real value. It remains with me now only as food for reflection. The deeper reflection is about how I am probably more like them than I wish to believe. I may not always act upon my desires, I may not always find a means to possess what I covet, and I may have more sophisticated rationalizations when I do, but the reflection illuminates some of my darker internal geography none the less. The theft of the camera is just my latest invitation into a conversation about all of us who take what is not ours.

I consider those who have stolen from me over the years. Wherever they are now living I pray that they are no longer stealing. I pray that they have found another, more abundant, path to covet. I pray that they have learned that nothing of any lasting value can be stolen. And, just before the "amen," I include myself in the prayer.

WAITING

The sight of bald children startles me into awareness that I have emigrated from my comfortable native land. The children possess a certain radiant beauty, the beauty of courage in the face of adversity, the beauty of hands securely held by loving parents, the beauty of life confronting death. If my motives were not subject to misinterpretation, I would have gladly hugged them and told them how beautiful they were. The option available to me is to admire in silent wonder as we pass in the foyer and the parking lot. By imagination, as a parent, I place myself at the entrance to the place where these parents and children live. I sighed a prayer, too deep for words, for their healing.

At the head of the wing where my father had his room we would pass a middle-aged woman in a hospital chair. Her legs were twisted by what I took to be a severe form of arthritis. The legs were obviously of no value for walking. The look on her face was vacant, except when I made eye contact with her she would return my smile. Her sounds were not speech we could understand. She would spend the day in her chair in the hall outside her room, silently watching the heedless parade. Her hunger for human contact was palpable. When I was a child, I remember my mother looking upon such affliction and speaking softly to herself: "poor soul."

Occasionally a plaintive voice would call from an adjacent room. It was a plea for attention, an impatient need waiting to be met, the after-effects of anesthesia or exasperation. A short visit is sufficient to invite exasperation in this foreign land. The voices without names and faces carry their need as surely as if they had both. Caring, over-worked staff responded to the voices as soon as they were able.

The medical center is a city of the un-well seeking wellness. It is a congregation of those gathered to offer and receive the blessings of the healing arts. By its nature and design it is focused primarily upon skillful medical art and science. It is a community of waiting; waiting for a doctor, waiting for a procedure to begin or finish, waiting for some word on what comes next, waiting for meals, waiting for a call to be returned, waiting for the surgeon to appear in scrubs with news of the surgery, waiting for the results of tests, waiting to be made well, waiting for release, waiting to live, waiting to die. Competent, compassionate medical professionals are doing the best they can with what they have. They travel with us as far down the road as the medical science shuttle will take us. And then we all wait to see what will happen after the door opens and we go our separate ways.

Waiting is one of the clearest realities of our lives. Everything that is important demands that we wait upon it. We wait to be born, to grow up, to finish school, to fall in love, to become well, to express our vocation, to stop our grieving, and to die. The waiting is a given. How we wait is another matter entirely. There are varieties of waiting.

The kind of waiting I experience at the medical center is of the anxious, uncertain variety. It is waiting for the unknown and the unknowable. We sit before a blank screen waiting for the movie to begin. We are aliens in this land. A foreign language is spoken. Our bodies, ourselves, become passive recipients. Abandon any hope of privacy or modesty. We are here to receive what is given, to demonstrate patience as patients, to participate in what we are offered so that we can "get well." Even when we receive the very best of care, there is more than one reason why we do not sleep well in this hotel.

There is another kind of waiting, however, with which we of the household of faith have a more intimate companionship. We are also waiting. But our waiting is different because we are positioned between two advents. We participate in a waiting that names us. We are waiting for some one rather than some thing. We are waiting for a completion and not a beginning. We are waiting for the return of a friend and not a stranger. We are waiting not in anxiety but in expectation, not in fear but in anticipation. St. Paul says In Romans that, "we ourselves, who have the first fruits of the Spirit, groan inwardly while we wait for adoption, the redemption of our bodies."[9]

We gratefully give thanks to God for the gift of the healing arts and for compassionate medical professionals. We could not imagine walking the road of illness without them. Sitting in the visitors' gallery of the medical center reminds me once again that waiting is a given. But I am also reminded that, even in our seasons of anxious waiting, we are not sitting before a blank screen. We are not waiting in the dark. We are not as those without hope. We are not waiting alone.

PACKING MERCIES

As an occasional visitor to different congregations, I have the pleasure of experiencing a variety of community worship. There are many similarities as well as significant differences. One element common to almost every service is the time before the prayers of the people when the community is invited to contribute their concerns and celebrations, or some variation on that theme. Prayer requests generally range from those for the personal needs in the congregation to a broad spectrum of those for the world parish. Everyone requests prayers for healing, consolation and traveling mercies for family and friends. Some also ask prayers for peace, food, justice, healing and blessings for God's children in other places.

One Sunday not so long ago the congregation was responding to the pastor's invitation to announce joys and concerns. Near the end of the time, a hand went up a few rows in front of me and a woman asked for "packing mercies." It was the pastor's spouse. The pastor had been appointed to a new congregation. The moving van would arrive in a few weeks. A ripple of knowing laughter skittered across the sanctuary.

Anyone who had ever moved understood the stress of changing an address. They knew the need for prayer if the family was to arrive at their new home without physical exhaustion and with some semblance of mental health. Military families, families who have hitched their career wagons to the corporate life and clergy households all contributed an understanding sympathetic sigh as we prayed together.

Her remark set my mind chasing after memories of the fourteen moves in my own odyssey. It was a moment of empathy that had roots in my own moves sustained by prayer as well as sweat and tears. The prayer request transported me to the tape dispensers, colored markers, newsprint bundles and dozens of sturdy cartons begged from the Wine and Spirits Shop. An unknowing visitor in the parsonage at either end of the move might well be startled by the colorful boxes that were formerly home to a variety of non-Wesleyan beverages.

The empties are filled, labeled, sealed and stacked, creating their own cardboard canyons on the first floor. Neglecting to label a box's contents is a serious omission that sets everyone adrift in a sea of ignorant searching at the destination. Where is the bread knife with the red handle? Where is my gray sweatshirt? Where are the coffee filters? Some household items hide so well that they only make their appearance on stage every other move.

One of the more useful skills I acquired along the way was household packing. To help pay the bills during graduate school days I worked for a moving company. Most pastors would benefit from an internship with a moving company. Packing should probably appear as an elective in the curriculum of our undergraduate colleges. In our society, most everyone gets some on-the-job training in the science and art of relocation. Most of us get to change our address several times along the way.

Packing and moving are among the most stressful stipulations in the fine print of the marriage covenant. In addition to the grief of saying goodbye to all of our support structures in a community, changing an address also rents a moving van of physical and emotional exhaustion. All members of the moving guild covet prayers for packing mercies. Family relationships and marriages submit to a season of final exams. Just to be a survivor of the experience merits a passing grade.

Moving does have its virtues, however. It can also be an occasion for taking stock of what we have accumulated, what we believe we will need to carry forward and what we may now need to set down. It is an opportunity to lighten the load. How to pack is not nearly as important a skill as discerning what to pack. It is a spiritual exercise as well as a physical one. In the many realms in which we make our home, less can be more.

Matthew reports that Jesus' traveling instructions to the disciples as he sent them to the house of Israel was that they travel very lightly: no gold, no copper, no bag, or two tunics, or sandals, or a staff.[10] Sounds like little more than the clothes on their backs. The monastic tradition insists upon poverty as well as chastity and obedience. The point seems to be that you need to set something down in order to take up something else. If you are full of one thing, then there is no room for anything else. This is radical stuff as well as good advice. It calls for a trust in divine providence that does not come to all of us along the way. No need to learn how to pack, just take very little. Take only what you really need.

In our culture, many of us have the burden of carrying too much. We are under continual re-construction, drafting blueprints for bigger barns. We watch the self-store villages springing up just outside of town. We need more and more space to house more and more things. The prospect of less makes us anxious. We devote much time, energy, and treasure to protect, maintain, insure, store and restore the things we own. Sometimes it seems like they really own us. Sometimes it seems like we end up serving them.

Navigating all the cardboard box canyons of our life, there are days when Jesus' instruction makes kingdom sense: the lighter the load, the longer you may travel. You have a better chance of getting to your destination if you carry less. We may be more useful along the way if there is more of us and less of other things. We can focus on what really matters if we set some things aside.

The impending arrival of the moving van may become just one particular spiritual exercise. An inventory of what we have, what we need and what we will carry forward is an opportunity to discern some truth about ourselves. We stand in need of packing mercies. Some of us are still trying to learn how to hold on with open hands.

ROAD RAGE

Class was in session. Although it was not a course for which I had registered, it was apparent that I had been expected. My name was called when attendance was taken. How do we inadvertently wander into these seminars? Is this the wrong classroom or the right one? It's often hard to know until you get to the first pop quiz.

Northbound near the I-81 intersections, I was suddenly aware that my life was in imminent danger. An 80 miles-per-hour motorized behemoth on my left was changing lanes at my expense. My Subaru no match for the Peterbilt, I yielded by brake and avoidance maneuver. Come right over, sir! Actually, in that moment of truth, other less charitable words and thoughts played center stage. Adrenalin poured from its hidden sources into my bloodstream and played a presto reveille for all my fight and flight responses. As the truck proceeded on its reckless course, now safely out of earshot of my pounding heart and trembling hands, I was able to observe what was happening in this lecture.

The tractor-trailer and a four-door sedan were engaged in an insane contest of killer-tag-road-rage initiated by a God-knows-what precipitating incident. The car actually tried to cut the truck off and then the truck returned the insult. Hostile arms, hands and digits were extended from windows to fuel the insanity. And so it went down the interstate, truck and car in mindless pursuit of each other, passing each other, cutting each other off, totally oblivious to the danger posed to innocents caught up in their macho madness. I hurled a prayer heavenward that the proverbial State Trooper would be at his post. I took perverse pleasure in rehearsing the multiple offenses that would appear on the citations. Big bucks! Big points! And that was just for starters. My racing heart was shouting "felony". Not all prayers, however, are answered in a fashion we might take to be timely.

The bizarre thrill show out of sight, I began to ponder what might have happened to get these two men so angry at each other that they were prepared literally to kill one another. That is not even to mention

144

that they were also fully prepared to kidnap a few unwilling spectators in the stands to participate in their interstate mayhem. What real or imagined highway slight could enflame egos to such reckless depths?

I moved inside the deeper recesses of my own shadow side and I began to think that most of us keep watch over a storeroom full of anger. We warehouse a reservoir of flammable emotion that feeds a small pilot light of anger and keeps it discretely burning on low. We hardly even notice the light and warmth the small flame casts. To all who care to take note we appear rational, integrated and balanced. But let a proper catalyst be tossed into the room and the destructive power of the resulting explosion can tear, shatter, and destroy that which cannot be put back together again. Our warehouse empties its contents in self-righteous justification to crush a real or imagined threat. We will take no prisoners, ourselves included.

From what I have seen, anger goes where we go. It is just some of what the Gardener insisted we pack as we were served the eviction notice in Eden. Since it seems to be original equipment in human experience the dilemma is what we are going to do with it. The writer of Ephesians seems to acknowledge that truth when admonishing, "Be angry but do not sin; do not let the sun go down on your anger, and do not make room for the devil."[11] The scriptures record anger that ignites fratricide on the one hand and anger that ignites the purification of the temple on the other. The behavior of Cain is vilified and the behavior of Jesus is admired.

Anger can be a tool for destruction or redemption. It depends upon the proper focus and appropriate application. Anger is a tool for villains and saints alike. Anger destroys or builds, enslaves or sets free, poisons or purifies.

The interstate classroom invited me to unlock my own warehouse and take an inventory of what I have stuffed there. I took some notes and set out to the curb a few items that I don't need any more. There is still plenty left, you understand. When I was exploring I noticed that some of that old stuff was really buried way back where it is hard to get at. I hope that when the catalyst is thrown on my pilot light the fuel that ignites will be anger without sin. I'll have to let you know after the first pop quiz.

ANGELS

Somewhere in the middle of the second decade of life, a syndrome of temporary forgetfulness overtakes many humans. Let us call it adolescent amnesia. The principal symptom of this amnesia is that the adolescent suddenly cannot remember that parents were the ones who brought him or her safely to that place of life. Youth cannot seem to recall that parents fed, clothed, sheltered, kissed abrasions, rocked through illness, charmed real and mythical monsters, changed diapers, drove to piano lessons, attended all concerts and games, took to Sunday School, taught the most valuable lessons of life by word and deed, and otherwise loved them as best they could for a dozen or so years. The memory is wiped clean by an invasion of mutant hormones.

How the adolescent thought that he or she got to that place in life without parents, they cannot say, except to be sure adults were not involved. Adolescents have empirical evidence to prove conclusively that parents know nothing at all and that they have gotten old without benefit of any adolescent experience of their own. Adolescents typically belong to the Groucho Marx School of Family Membership, which is to say they do not want to belong to any family that would have them for a member.

Moreover, if our parents know nothing, then our friends know everything. Peers are the omniscient instructors. All standards of taste, dress, demeanor, values, language, and ambition are imported from those who are as mystified as we are. Adolescence is a kind of pick-up seminar where clueless amnesiacs try to find the way forward without reference to the adult world around them.

It is a time of life when many of us awaken one morning to find ourselves among strangers, probably dropped off in a wicker basket on the porch years ago, raised by these well-meaning but abysmally ignorant folks, who may someday tell us about our true family. My family does not understand me and probably does not even love me. We stand at the entrance to adolescence like a well-meaning visitor from another planet waiting for instructions. In time, we usually find our way home.

I was not aware of it then, but adolescent visa in hand, some adults had taken notice of me. I was a member of a small band of guerrillas who attended the church school at First Church every Sunday. We were there for a battle of wits and endurance with a cast of saintly characters. They were members blessed with an abundance of patience, mercy, forbearance, long-suffering, and kindness. We callow fellows always assumed that we got the best of these battles. However, in retrospect, the saints always won the day because we, having failed to turn them permanently against us, were always welcomed back again next Sunday. In spite of our best efforts, they refused to abandon us.

The most influential non-parent adults in my adolescence were some optimists in that congregation. They gently and persistently entered my life, assuming a role in my Christian nurture, or more to the point, my reclamation. However, it was not done in any way obvious enough to arouse adolescent defenses. By a subtle process of invitation and affirmation, they drew me into a circle that welcomed me and encouraged me to develop; using the gifts they believed I had, even though they were invisible to me.

That initiation into a family of youth and adults blessed me with friendships I still cherish decades later. I learned the life and language of that family, experiencing the fellowship of those for whom Christian Faith mattered. My parents were delighted, but wise enough not to say so.

Those adults not only noticed me but also modeled for me the fullness of a life in faith. Enticed into a wonderful association of young people and adults, we worked together, laughed together, ate together, sang together, played together, worshipped together, and traveled together. They witnessed before me the richness, joy and peace of an authentic Christian life, making that life both desirable and attainable.

I am afraid the word "angel" is used far too glibly today. Unfortunately, the word is informed more by Hollywood than by scripture. However, it is difficult for me to find a more appropriate word to describe the laity who nurtured me. They were watching over me, guiding me, mentoring me, educating me, loving me, seeing things in me that I could not see myself, believing that God was calling me and helping me to hear that call. It any case, it is holy work, the work of the saints, to help a young person find God within himself or herself and within a community of faith. To mentor young people is a vocation worthy of any of us, worthy of all of us.

Along the way, I am overwhelmed by my indebtedness to those saints. I am awed by the mystery of finding myself in their faithful, loving care at just the right time.

In honor of Grace Rose

CHASING PEAS

On my usual commute between home and almost anywhere else I drive a rural byway beside a section of single-family housing. Some of it is privileged and some of it is modest. One home of the latter variety is of the so-called "mobile" type, a curious name since I am convinced it has never changed address since the day that it was set upon its cinder blocks a generation ago. The dwelling is a chronic eye magnet. As I climb the gradual incline in front of the store-bought dwelling, my eye involuntarily shifts to the right to take in the curious sight.

The home is obviously out of level. From front to back there is a drop of what I would guess to be about twelve or fifteen inches, perhaps more. It appears level from side to side, but the back length of the house is noticeably down the hill from the front. There are folks living here all the while. The yard is well kept. The house itself is an older model but in no way decrepit or neglected.

I try to imagine what it would be like to face the challenges of living in this house. Is all of the furniture blocked to level or have they just adjusted to the declination? Must chairs have the wheels removed to prevent unannounced travel? I imagine chasing peas across the dinner plate before they escape to the table or floor. Such speculation regularly kidnaps my imagination, and I take a side excursion into the decline house.

Lumber, tools, and other building materials recently appeared in the front yard. Subsequently, there were further signs that workers would be making some amendments to the modest structure. "Finally," I thought, "they are going to set the house foursquare." Perhaps the family had been prudently saving funds in order to make this correction. I suspected they had taken about as much life on the decline as they could tolerate.

As I watched the construction gradually progress, I was puzzled. Apparently, the family had decided to replace their small entrance awning with a contractor-build porch on the front of the house. An attractive and well-constructed covered porch now adds an all-weather

149

entrance and some additional outdoor living space for the occupants. The porch appears foursquare. The addition completed, I now assumed that they would raise the rear of the home to match the level of the new entrance area, making one unified whole, a merger of old and new, true and even: on the level.

It did not happen. The workers packed their tools and took their leave when the porch was completed. I waited in vain for work to begin on leveling the house. I still wait. Visitors can now be welcomed on a level porch before they enter the house when everything heads downhill. It is a mystery and a wonder. There must be a story that, if only I knew it, would make the decline house comprehensible.

Given enough time, most of us seem to be able to accommodate ourselves to almost any situation. Our ability to accommodate is both blessing and liability. In Philippians, when St. Paul speaks of learning "to be content with whatever I have," he points to a reservoir of spiritual strength that sustains him whatever life presents.[12] However, we know from the whole of his ministry that he did not intend that as license to collaborate with evil. Discerning the difference between contentment and collaboration is a continuous prayerful effort. It is God's answer to the familiar Serenity petition about "wisdom to know the difference."

My own natural inclination is to amend the tilting structures of my life by adding something extra. Usually, I am perfectly, painfully, aware that I am living on a slope, part of me having settled or sunk. My usual attempt to come to rights is by building a new porch to attach to the existing structure. It feels good to have that level entrance, it makes an agreeable impression on those who pass by, and it might even, from some perspectives, hide what is not foursquare. However, when I step inside my own house peas still roll off the plate. I still stumble into the wall if I don't mind my step.

I notice as well that what is personal is also expressed in the various institutions, ecclesiastical, social, and political, that comprise our lives. We suffer all the time with what is broken in the lives of the various families to which we belong. When we rouse ourselves to make some change, we typically build a new porch on the structure, hoping that it will bring the whole dwelling to the level. We find ourselves adding porches upon porches upon entrances. We decorate the house, add some landscaping, replace the windows, and pave the driveway. However, the level and the plumb line refuse to be co-conspirators. We still lose our balance and bump into walls. Peas still roll off the plate.

It costs significantly more to bring a house to level than to add a porch. There is not only the outer excavation, jacking and blocking, but, once done, all life inside the house will need to adjust to a new reality. Fundamental change is expensive, the final cost not usually specified in the construction contract. There is, however, an even higher cost to be paid when we accommodate ourselves to life on the tilt.

The good news upon which we stake our lives pretty much dismisses cosmetic improvement out of hand. We are invited to allow God to build a new foundation upon which to anchor the truth of our lives. Without the fundamental change which grace empowers, we spend our lives in the hands of one sub-contractor or another, tinkering with appearances, living on the tilt, chasing peas across the table.

COFFEE BREAK

It's time for a break. It is past time to stretch the legs and take on fuel for the balance of the trip. The turnpike rest stop is a welcome midway between departure and arrival. It also serves my favorite brand of Italian coffee, freshly brewed caffeine being my lifelong drug of choice.

I am prepared with thermal travel mug, anticipating the pleasure of a medium black, no sugar, to pacify the withdrawal symptoms. The queue is short; one person precedes me. He places his order and waits to receive his beverage. He is a large man, serious, severe-looking even. He impresses me as the kind of fellow who rolls his own. Without any preliminaries, receipt in hand he turns and, in a voice obviously intended for ears in addition to mine, says, "Isn't that the most ridiculous thing you ever saw? $4.11 for a cup of coffee! It's crazy."

There is no trace of humor or irony in his voice. I am a bit startled because, since the prices are posted, I have reason to assume that he ordered what he wanted and was prepared to pay. Is it just a case of buyer's remorse? I am beginning to wish that the line were a bit longer and I were further back. Why me, Lord? The man is very angry, perhaps on the edge of losing control. He continues,

"It's the same thing everywhere. It's ridiculous. The whole world is going nuts. Everywhere you turn someone is ripping you off. You want to hear something crazy? I was in Texas recently and I saw a huge sign that reads, 'SLICK WILLY'S FAMILY POOL HALL'. Can you tell me how in hell there can be such a thing as a "family pool hall?"

He was becoming louder and more agitated. I was becoming increasingly uneasy. What had I stumbled upon? My imagination comes on line and I begin to wonder if this might be one of those situations where a firearm appears and the world turns upside down. I make eye contact with the man and acknowledge his comments with

152

occasional nods, trying to be present in an invisible way, feigning non-anxious presence.

His coffee finally arrives. He takes it and stomps out the door, voicing his disgust and disapproval about far more than his mochaccino. I hope he finds that his beverage exceeds his expectations. He could surely use some happy surprise to ameliorate his frustration and rage. I ponder what he might do with that anger on the highway.

Our world is afloat on a sea of anger. I would like to believe that we are all traveling in a seaworthy vessel, but I strongly suspect we are just adrift in a life raft. I sit in a darkened cinema awaiting the main feature and find myself awash in a twenty-minute cloudburst of gratuitously violent "trailers" announcing what is coming soon. The number of movies of the "revenge" genre overwhelms me. Innocent blood is spilled and official or vigilante vengeance refills the cup to overflowing. Movies about psychopaths make big money. It is just "entertainment" but it plays music within us.

We are in the mood just now for some getting even, some comeuppance, some pay back, some settling accounts, some cleaning house, and some retributive justice. We know the source of some of our anger. We feel powerless to fix the things that we believe are broken. We feel fully justified, even righteous, in our blood lust. The Christian community is not exempt, in some quarters actually providing the theological rationale for retribution rather than redemption.

We come to our anger honestly. Our Garden brothers instructed us in fratricide. As a family, we have learned the lesson well, raising violence to a high art, perfecting both means and motive. Even all four Gospels remember an incident of Jesus' anger when he "drove out" the moneychangers and animal sellers from the temple.[13] There are few of us who cannot put contemporary names to moneychangers and animal sellers. Although the Gospel writers do not say so, I sometimes imagine that the overturned tables and broken animal cages were soon set aright and it was business as usual once Jesus was out of sight.

The writer of Colossians admonishes his community to purge that which is incompatible with a resurrected life: anger, wrath, malice, slander, and abusive language.[14] It is a first century primer on anger management. Anger can be dangerous to our community life as well as our soul. A wise person once observed that when we sit down at the banquet table of anger we generally discover that we are the main course. Unleashed anger often fixes things that are not broken.

Yet, anger has its place with the rest of our emotions, a rightful seat at the table in the community of faith, a rightful place on the agenda of Christian conferencing. Anger, rightly understood and wisely applied, can be a powerful force for change. Anger is an appropriate and proper response to injustice, bigotry, human abuse, idolatry, oppression, and violence. Without anger, we run the risk of passivity, the risk of being co-opted by the evil of the world, the risk of baptizing sin and calling it tolerance, and the risk of making a mockery of forgiveness.

Our family of faith serves by providing an opportunity for us to talk about what makes us angry and why. Together we can discern what God is trying to say to us in our anger. We can listen to that anger as an instrument of revelation. Together, we can find ways to keep the moneychangers and animal sellers from setting up shop again once Jesus is out of sight.

FENCES

I always believed that I knew a fence when I saw one. After all, in my rural zip code fences are a standard feature of many yards. There are fences to keep dogs and children corralled. There are fences to keep the relatives of Bambi and Thumper from the chard. There are fences to mitigate wind-driven snow. There are fences that give permission for Morning Glories, Clematis, beans, cucumbers and peas to get a grip as they stretch sunward.

Over my dashboard, driving out of town, I watch a new fence under construction. However, I soon began to wonder what purpose has set this project in motion. What would motivate this fellow to invest so much labor in such a serious barrier? Day by day it grows to fifty yards from road to woods. It is seven feet high, an additional two-foot amendment wired to the original five to give it a prodigious height. All I can imagine is that it intends to keep whitetails from their midnight buffet in his broccoli. But with that height, I am now picturing Bullwinkle more than Bambi.

What really kidnapped my attention, however, was the observation that the fence had only one dimension: road to woods. A garden fence with only one side would deter no deer, raccoon, rabbit, or woodchuck. Even intellectually challenged wildlife would merely walk around and graze on the other side, perhaps using the fence as a backscratcher. I watch the progress each day as I crest the hill to see where this will all end. I keep waiting for the appearance of the other sides of the fence that will create an enclosure. Finally, the homeowner and his tools take their leave with only a single line of fence standing.

It is clear that this fence was not designed to keep anything either in or out. The fence was a billboard erected to convey some angry message to the man's immediate neighbor. It was a sign of the enmity between them. I can only guess what real or imagined offense captured the man's time, energy, and money for such a useless barrier. I can only imagine his satisfaction when he opens his curtains and sees the fruit of this labor. I can only speculate what the fenced-out neighbors feel as they mow their lawns along opposite sides of the galvanized divide.

A well-known Robert Frost aphorism linking quality fences and quality neighbors specifies "good" fences. Could this in any sense be a good fence? I am trying to make my way back from the answer to the question. When a fence is the answer, fear or anger is generally part of the question.

Many of us remember both the construction and destruction of the Berlin wall. A wall is a fence with an exclamation point. Even as the sound of that falling wall still reverberates in our ears, another wall is under construction in the land where Jesus walked. And a fence has a mission of separation on the southern border of our own land. Fences are a regular feature of the landscape east of Eden.

We are soon to enter an interminable, angry season in which political parties will try to convince us to join them on their side of the fence in order to keep the other side from power. Fear is distributed indiscriminately and extravagantly. Words became the "no trespassing" signs hung upon those barriers: conservative, liberal, gay, straight, black, white, terrorist, freedom-fighter, war, peace, patriot, traitor, saved, lost, clean, unclean, them, us. We build the barriers with tools wielded in clinched fists. Such fences seduce us into a cul-de-sac of self-righteousness. *Caveat emptor*: fences imprison as well as protect.

In addition to a lighted candle, new clothing, and a certificate, one additional gift that we should give to everyone at their baptism is a sack of hand tools: hammer, saw, wire cutters, and wrecking bar. The baptized life is one of both building up and tearing down. There are bridges to build and walls to demolish. Our baptism unites us with the One who has "broken down the dividing wall of hostility"[15] and has given us "the ministry of reconciliation."[16] Part of growing in grace is learning to discern when it is time to break down and when to build up.

A one-sided rural fence sets me to imagining a day when I might get to see the neighbors on both sides of that "good neighbor" fence out there together in the sunshine, sharing tools, laughing as they dismantle that useless barrier. Unlikely that may be, but I smile as I hope such a happy scene.

But that new spite fence also serves to remind me about some of my own unfinished business. It gets me to remembering that there are still some anger and fear fences in my own life. There are self-righteous walls upon which I have labored long with grim determination and clenched fists. I have my own one-sided fences to demolish. I have my own useless walls to tear down. It is time to open that neglected box with the baptism tools inside.

GOSPEL ECONOMICS

It is a smack upside the head: "Lotto Jackpot Now $17 Million." National economic crisis or no, gaming remains a recession-proof way to pay some of the government's bills. The billboard beckons to one and all on the interstate. Generally I don't even see it. Today it kidnaps me and takes me to a part of town where I don't generally venture after dark. I begin to imagine how much money we are actually talking about. That would be 17 followed by six zeroes. Even someone numerically-challenged knows that we are talking real money here.

My mind begins to imagine what I could do with that kind of wealth. A siren knocks and I open the door and set an extra place at the table. Even after I care for the needs of my Uncle Sam, there would be money and enough to get some things done: good things, wonderful things, render-unto-God things. Sweet Jesus, I am ready to buy a ticket and book passage on that cruise ship.

I begin to imagine what a huge endowment would mean to the holy work of people and places I care deeply about: hungry, homeless and hapless. I smile to think what I could do to add some security to a little Christian School on the West Bank in Israel that opens its doors of education to the needy, Christian or Muslim. My brain reels and I smile at the difference my lucre could make, the joy I could bring, the rescue I could affect, and the ministry I could purchase. I think that if I give it all away I would be left with nothing but peace of mind. Some pocket change would be enough for me. God knows, I would be happy to do it anonymously.

It is a complete fantasy, of course. I don't play Lotto or take overnight trips with any of that fraternity. I am offended that our government panders to our hope. I resent that what is most precious is priced so cheaply. That does not even take into account the reality that we have about as much chance of winning this game played with house rules as we have of being abducted by extraterrestrials. Instead of challenging us to share, we are enticed to get, not by using our gifts

158

of body and brain but by the fickle whim of ping-pong balls. What kind of house can you build on the false hopes of the needy?

Reality notwithstanding, I ascend the gangplank to the ship. Harmless enough on a morning ride to town I suppose, but my journey reveals something of a deeper desire, a persistent heart-longing of those who dream of Shangri-la or Arcadia. Although we know full well it will most likely turn out to be like the man behind the curtain in Oz. It is a reverie rooted in the hope of "more." If only I had more, then I would have enough, then I would be satisfied and then I could afford to be generous.

It is the ancient, new-every-morning myth of happiness by addition. I don't believe that I believe it, but that doesn't stop me from imagining it. I must partially believe it because my daydreams betray me. If only I had that money I could do more and better. Of course, it flies in the face of the other truth by which I claim to live. Caught between what I say and what I dream I wish this ship would dock and let me to slip quietly ashore when the crew is sleeping.

What I say I believe is an opposite truth: the Gospel call of abundant life by subtraction. It calls to mind St. Paul speaking in Philippians of Jesus "emptying himself."[17] We have no evidence of which I am aware that Jesus ever sought to acquire anything. Everything was borrowed: stable, loaves and fishes, donkey, upper room, cross and tomb. His life force was broadcast, subtracted, and left behind as he lived. There is less of him so there can be more of others. It is the model of the servant. He invites, "follow me." I recall that John Wesley left behind little more than a few teaspoons and a movement.

There is a daily fork in the road. Worn smooth is the way of addition: life measured by accumulation. The road less traveled, on the other hand, is littered with what has been set down, given away and thrown aside by those with empty hands and full hearts. But that is not the prevailing wind blowing in our culture. It never will be. It is foolish and incomprehensible. It is the way to be taken up only by those who have taken Gospel Economics 101: life measured by what is left behind.

Moving on down the interstate, the lotto invitation fades from view as another reality takes up residence in the passenger seat. I will never win the Lotto. What I will be able to leave behind I already have. My life is expressed both by what I embrace and what I renounce. It is unfaithful to hold out for better terms.

GROWING MEDIUM

I t is an eye-magnet on the road into town. Everyone knows Ray's garden. It is the gold standard for summer vegetables. We watch and learn what we should be doing. Except under cover of snow, there is always something to learn at Ray's. Ray knows humus.

The rich dark loam did not just happen. It is by Ray's effort over many years that he now has the soil to grow wondrous vegetables. We watch the compost and manure arrive in the spring and fall. We watch the rye cover-crop planted after the final harvest. We watch him with the Troy-Built amalgamating all the top layers into the deep. It is impossible not to smile as we observe all the magic in plain sight. You could put a stick in Ray's garden, and it would grow. A thumb turns green by dint of art and science. The art and science are bound together with sweat. The rich harvest begins in the fertile soil.

If you are a gardener, you know what humus is. It is that rich organic material that has the power to change dirt into soil. It is why gardeners are so interested in compost. It is why we recycle leaves and grass and plants and kitchen waste and allow them slowly to decompose. What comes from that process is a dark, moist, rich substance that has all of the nutrients that produce terrific tomatoes, stunning snap peas, beautiful broccoli, and succulent squash.

The word humility comes from the same root as the word humus. Humble is not so much what we do as what we are. We become humble by being like humus. We become the soil in God's garden. God plants the seeds, waters and weeds. God provides the sun and the warmth. The seed grows silently and mysteriously within us. The seed grow and matures. As it grows, we become more and more the way God intends.

To be the rich soil in which God is growing means that I no longer need to be number one. I no longer need to scramble to get a place at the head table. I no longer need to believe that I am better than other people. I no longer need to win all the time. I no longer need to take offense when people do not respect me as I think I deserve. I no longer need to put any other person or ethnic or racial group down as being inferior to me. I toss it in the compost pile.

Humility means that I believe I am already sitting in the place of honor. I am already secured in the place where I am. My security is not based upon what other people think or say about me or where I sit at the head table. Being humble, means we are content to be fertile ground for God to grow.

The parable of the Pharisee and the Publican points the way.[18] The problem with the Pharisee was not that he was a holy man who kept all the religious laws. That's all well and good. The problem was that the Pharisee was so filled with himself that there was no room for God. His prayer was nothing but self congratulation. He does not need God. His prayer is nothing but providing God with non-incriminating information about his holy life. God would have a hard time entering the Pharisee's heart. The Pharisee is full already.

The tax collector stands as someone in need. He brings little more to God than his need and his brutal self-knowledge. He knows himself, not for what he has, but for what he needs. His heart is a particularly fertile place for God to plant and to grow a new life.

I have sometimes wondered what Jesus meant when he said that those who humble themselves will be "exalted." I don't see how it can mean that the humble will get to sit in the places of honor. I don't believe that the humble will get in line ahead of the arrogant. I can't believe that the humble will get rich or famous. Jesus was never interested in any of those things.

I believe that "exalted" means that the humble already have everything that they need. They can sit anywhere. They can wait patiently in line. They can let others go first. They already live in the place of honor. They are in the garden. In fact, they are the garden.

The ones who know their need are the rich, dark, deep, fertile soil in which God is growing. With deep roots and strong branches they faithfully wait while the fruits of the spirit mature, until the Gardner comes and brings the final harvest home.

In honor of Raymond Roese

LUNACY

The right turn off the rural two-lane blacktop dips from SR/590 and winds around the Curtis Reservoir. It twists sharply and then steeply climbs Reservoir Road between silage corn fields. I am not far from home. Having made this run thousands of times, I am not particularly in the moment as dusk covers the fields. It is all the more startling then to crest the hill and be confronted by an enormous full moon lightly resting on the horizon. I pull to the grassy shoulder and turn the engine off. It is an invitation into hyperbole. It is a voice from a burning bush addressing me in a language I have heard before – take off your shoes, remove your hat, genuflect, be still and know.

It is a conspiracy between my eyes, brain and the moon on the horizon. Evidently the moon is the same size regardless of its placement in the night sky. The astronomers say it is an optical illusion that makes the moon just appear to be as large as it is before me now. The science is quickly overcome, however, by the aesthetic.

The full moon claims me like nothing else in the night sky. I am over the moon, as it were. My calendar is marked each month for the date of the full moon as well as the name assigned by one of the Native Peoples. When I send email messages to friends I will often call attention to the particular full moon we happen to be enjoying. It is the celestial event that will have its say within me month upon month upon year. I brake for the full moon, Flower, Wolf, Harvest, Cold, Worm and Blue, basking in its reflected light, savoring the greatest show on earth, and sad at its waning. Where I live the full moon on a clear night is a flood light which invites the world to glow from within.

Standing before Vincent Van Gogh's *Rain,* painted during his stay at the Saint-Paul-de Mausolee Clinic in 1889, I am likewise captured. It is not a moon this time but it is another invitation into transcendence, seeing the invisible through the artist's eyes. Van Gogh sees for the rest of us. It is the transcendence of Casals playing a Bach Cello Suite. Casals hears for the rest of us. It is the transcendent night call of wolves or the deep water song of the humpbacks in a language we wish we could understand. The wolves and humpbacks speak for the rest of us.

These are the moments to give thanks for the privilege of being a human being here in the garden. We open our eyes or ears and we bond with a truth beyond words. They are the moments of uninvited joy, captured by we know not what, when a curtain is briefly pulled aside and the universe permits us a glimpse, the art transparent to the artist.

Apparently the moon was a suspicious thing to our ancestors, if the root meaning of lunacy is to be believed. Emergency workers, usually with a smile, will repeat the urban legend that suggests a positive correlation between the full moon and calls to 911. While I have always considered that relationship a bit fanciful, it does come to mind in the roadside sanctuary as I am captured by the view through my windshield.

The moon as new age icon or as raw material for astrology has nothing to say to me. I am far more amazed by the astronomy of it all. I know the basic geology and astrophysics, but even with that this moon on the brow of the hill is not a science lecture. It captures my attention, imagination and wonder not by what I know, but by all that I am still learning. What the moon usually retrieves from my memory is some of Psalm 8:

When I look at your heavens, the work of your fingers, the moon and the stars that you have established, what are human beings that you are mindful of them, mortals that you should care for them?[19]

I feel a bond with the psalmist who ponders the night sky for universal connections and with St. Francis who rehearses the Psalmist's wonder:

Be praised, my Lord, through Sister Moon and the stars; in the heavens you have made them bright, precious and beautiful.[20]

The moon points beyond itself to its source – the creation in praise of the creator. Because of the change in perspective the moon now appears to grow smaller as it rises. I am aware of the moon illusion once again. The aesthetic recedes in favor of the science. It is time to get on home. Once again I have been reminded of things that I know very deeply. I have been reminded of things that I do not even know yet.

NOTES

Introduction

    1. Matthew 20:1ff

Advent and Christmas

    1. Luke 7:18-23
    2. "O Little Town of Bethlehem," Phillips Brooks, 1868.
    3. Lawrence Ferlinghetti, "Christ Climbed Down," *A Coney Island of the Mind* (New York: New Directions Books, 1958), 69-70

Epiphany

    1. Matthew 2:1-12
    2. Philippians 4:8
    3. Neil Postman, *Amusing Ourselves to Death* (New York: Penguin Books, 1985).
    4. Luke 2:8-20
    5. Matthew 2:1-12

Lent

    1. Matthew 3:13ff
    2. Mark 1:12
    3. Philippians 2:6-11
    4. John 12:12-19
    5. Luke 19:41-44
    6. I Corinthians 11:23-26
    7. Psalm 51
    8. Isaiah 53:4-5
    9. The event is remembered by Dante Negro, then the Concert Manager for the Brooklyn Center for the Performing Arts, who attended the Horowitz rehearsal. Negro's papers are in the archives of the Brooklyn College Library.

10. Luke 23:44-45
11. Psalm 139:11-12
12. John 19:30

Easter

1. John 11:1ff
2. John 12:1ff
3. John 10:22ff
4. John 20:1-18
5. John 20: 19-24

Pentecost

1. Luke 12:49
2. "Where Shall My Wondering Soul Begin," the eight-stanza hymn written by Charles Wesley about his conversion on May 21, 1738 and believed to be the hymn sung by John, Charles and the congregation on the night of John's conversion May 24, 1738.
3. Journal of John Wesley for May 24, 1738.
4. Simone Weil, *Waiting for God* (New York: Harper Perennial Modern Classics, 2009), 59.
5. II Corinthians 5:16-17

Ordinary Time: All in the Family

1. Matthew 6:3-4
2. Luke 6:38
3. "Hymn of Promise," Natalie Sleeth, 1986
4. John 15:4 (The Jerusalem Bible, 1966)
5. Galatians 6:9-10
6. Martin Luther, "A Mighty Fortress Is Our God," stanza 3
7. Governor Carroll Campbell, Jr., South Carolina State of the State Address, January 17, 1990.
8. Martin Luther, "A Mighty Fortress Is Our God," stanza 1
9. John 6:22

10. John 6:25-26
11. I Corinthians 4:10
12. Frederick Buechner, "Fool," *Wishful Thinking* (New York: Harper and Row, 1973), 32.
13. Hebrews 12:1

Ordinary Time: On the Road

1. Jean Giono, *The Man Who Planted Trees,* 1953.
2. Matthew 25:31ff
3. Luke 16:19-31
4. John 6:68
5. Deuteronomy 30:15ff
6. Psalm 121: 5-6
7. Matthew 19:18; Mark 10:19; Luke 18:20
8. Romans 2:21
9. Romans 8:22ff
10. Matthew 10:9
11. Ephesians 4:26-27
12. Philippians 4:11
13. Matthew 21:12-13; Mark 11:15-17; Luke 19:45-46; John 2: 14-16.
14. Colossians 3:8
15. Ephesians 2:14
16. II Corinthians 5:18-19
17. Philippians 2:7
18. Luke 18:9ff
19. Psalm 8:3ff
20. St. Francis of Assisi, "The Canticle of the Sun."

CPSIA information can be obtained at www.ICGtesting.com
Printed in the USA
BVOW011843301112

306851BV00001B/4/P